Work Hard and Get Ahead

Career Paths Vol. 3: 31 Tips on How To Excel at Work

James Bellerjeau

A Fine Idea

Contents

Introduction

G reetings readers and congratulations! Simply by virtue of being here, you are already on the path to increasing your odds of success.

There is nothing worse than putting in the work and failing to progress in one's career. Here we explore the reasons why some types of hard work pay off, while others leave you tired but no further.

We will also examine alternative paths to the top, relying on tactics and pragmatism more than simply putting in the hours. Although we face similar challenges in the workplace, we each have different abilities, and knowing how to leverage our particular strengths is useful.

In a perfect world, everyone would find a place that suits them well. They would have well-meaning colleagues and understanding bosses. In the real world, where we all spend our days, we have to deal with competitive colleagues and clueless bosses. That's no obstacle for the savvy employee, prepared by the lessons contained here.

You will find additional approaches to succeeding at work in the companion volumes **Thriving at Work** and **The Pragmatist's Rules for Work**.

Success at work is not necessarily the same as how to live a good life or achieve satisfaction. If you want to explore these topics more deeply, I recommend you spend some time with the **Pragmatic Wisdom** series.

Be well.

Chapter One

The Back-Door Path to Success

You don't need to take outsized risks to get outsized results. It's better to be unassuming but unstoppable

We are impressed by outsized results. It is not surprising that we are captivated by surprising events:

- The school dropout who starts an internet company and becomes a billionaire

- The trader who comes out the winner on a gigantic bet

- The video that goes viral on its way to 100 million views

Because we are so frequently confronted with such examples, we are at great risk of overestimating their likelihood.

What we see represents the tiniest fraction, the results of billions of experiments and attempts. From 100 million tweets, a handful will capture the public's roving eye. Most fall quietly, unremarked.

Multitudes pass by unnoticed, while the few successes grab all our rapt attention.

What does it say when we pursue highly unlikely things?

What does it say for a person to pursue a strategy if they have a 99% chance of failure? Consider a person who is facing a million-to-one odds.

At what point do we look beyond the size of the potential payoff to question our investment in the project?

Experience with U.S. state lotteries is instructive. Someone wins each lottery, and because there are so many lotteries, states announce new lottery winners frequently.

Never mind that in large lotteries your odds fall to *100 million to one* or worse of winning. Yes, "someone's gotta win," as the lottery marketers remind us. But for one person to win, many millions must lose.

Consider the other losers in the lottery of life: the school dropout who *didn't* become a billionaire, the video that has but 24 views, and the trader who was on the wrong side of that bet.

This is not an argument against trying to do unlikely things. But it helps to understand your odds before you bet the house.

Then there are the people who take outsize risks and get away with it, for a time:

- Think of investment banks that earn profits for years by making large bets with borrowed money and then lose it all when markets move unexpectedly.

- Consider the base jumper or free climber. They may have successfully summited and descended a hundred times, until the one time they don't.

At what point do we consider an inveterate risk-taker to be safely home with their gains intact?

You can achieve large gains without taking large risks

Today I suggest to you there is an alternative approach to achieving great things.

It's not one you'll see headlining the news or discussed in online forums. But it is much more likely to put the odds in your favor.

To play this alternative approach, you don't need huge luck on your side or deep-pocketed investors. You need only draw upon something that you already have: **patience**.

Let me explain.

Slow, steady, incremental progress is quiet and, by definition, not flashy. The magic and the power lie in consistency.

- Start somewhere, anywhere, and move in the direction of your choosing. A single step will suffice.

- Then tomorrow, do it again. And again.

Whether your desire is to save money, improve your fitness, or become wise, you can make progress incrementally. You just need to have the patience to keep going.

Think of yourself like Kobayashi Issa's snail:

O snail
Climb Mount Fuji
But slowly, slowly!

This is such excellent advice. It applies on an individual level and on a business level.

Think how many once high-flying companies had their moment and crashed back down when unrealistic expectations met harsh reality. Founders who reached for the sun, only to fall short as the great majority do.

Slow and steady is the path less traveled

Do not mistake me. I am not advising you to give up outrageous goals.

I am urging you to use the little-traveled path up the back of the mountain to your goal.

- You will not reach the summit in a week, true.

- But you will travel farther and higher than almost everyone who makes the frontal assault.

It takes discipline and conviction to stay true to a slow but steady course. Particularly when you're regularly confronted with examples of instant success.

You will doubt and you will waver. If you have chosen a goal worth pursuing and are taking steps reasonably designed to get you there, then you are already successful.

Stay on the path. You don't need to take outsized risks to get outsized results. It's better to be unassuming but unstoppable.

Be well.

Chapter Two

Can You Succeed at Work Without Working Hard?

The reason people do not succeed on the basis of hard work alone is partly due to luck, but also, partly due to misplaced priorities

You're busy, so here is the answer right up front: *It's complicated.*

Succeeding at work without breaking a sweat isn't impossible, but there are a few hurdles to overcome before you get to the "work smarter, not harder" point.

I know people who achieved success without appearing to work hard. They are in a tiny minority. But I will also tell you hard work is no guarantee of success.

"Yikes! Are you telling us that hard work is likely necessary for success, but that working hard does not mean we'll be successful?"

Don't despair. Stay with me for a few minutes, and I will tell you what I learned about working hard in over 80,000 hours of doing it. You may be able to avoid some of my mistakes.

I am a big believer in the power of continuous improvement and habits. You don't need to take giant steps to achieve big progress. Small steps taken consistently over time will add up to large results.

One way to take actions consistently is to make them into a habit.

Not all habits are good for you

We call harmful habits "vices," which otherwise means moral faults or weaknesses, and include in this category things like drinking alcohol, smoking, or eating too much chocolate.

Where does working hard fall on the spectrum of virtue and vices?

For a long time, I considered hard work to be a clear virtue. Not only that, being able to work intensely for long periods of time is a great competitive advantage at work.

Particularly with a steady stream of new workers coming along who have chronically short attention spans, a person who is able to stay focused on a task and work on it until they have made progress or completed it is well-equipped to succeed.

I am aware there is a strong counter-current to this work-hard ethos. Browse the self-help aisle, and you will find best-selling books advising you to learn "How Not to Give a F*ck" and the like.

Similar articles in mainstream publications explain the danger of associating too much with your work and the harm this can have on your happiness and health. Being a workaholic is not a good thing.

Now with some time and distance from my last senior management role, I have come to two realizations that I will share with you:

- Working hard is a key factor contributing to your success in almost any endeavor.

- Working hard is itself habit-forming, even as it crosses the line from virtue over to harmful vice.

What happened to me in working so many hours all those years is that my ability to work long hours became part of who I was and what I did. Not only that, I learned how to make each of those hours count more than most people's by focusing relentlessly on effectiveness and productivity, not just hours at my desk.

Do you know how much time most people waste on unproductive activities each day? Simply by avoiding wasted time, you can become massively more productive than the average employee.

Add to that focusing on carefully chosen strategic targets, and then working harder than your colleagues, and you become highly effective. Unstoppable, really.

You will always outcompete someone who is not willing to put in the same time as you. I refer not just to hours spent working, but learning how not to waste time, and how to productively use the time you have focused on the right priorities.

Here it is, the real answer

The reason people do not succeed on the basis of hard work alone is partly due to luck, but also, partly due to misplaced priorities.

You can be extremely busy putting out fires and responding to urgent tasks. To make your hard work pay off, it needs to be directed to your own priorities.

If you work in a larger organization, your priorities must align with your company's. But that still leaves a lot of room for you to work on more and less helpful topics.

Working hard will not necessarily make you happy. As noted, more people are realizing that done unthinkingly, hard work will make you miserable.

I have lots of thoughts about how to achieve happiness and satisfaction in your life. Success at work is one path, but you must not assume that hard work by itself will bring you fulfillment.

It has taken me a long time, years actually, to break my habit of working long hours. After all, it was a key factor in my success, so why should I lose the habit? As with any habit, after a certain point, it becomes easier to just continue it than to question why you are doing it.

This is because if you question your long-held habits, you also question the foundation of your choices. "Was I a fool to work so hard for so long? What did it bring me?"

The reason for me to ultimately seek a different balance, if not lose the habit of work entirely, was because I decided that success at work was not the only yardstick I would use to measure my progress. I wanted happiness and satisfaction in life.

I leave you with this thought: Even if breaking a habit would cause you to question the validity of your earlier choices, is that really worse than continuing on a path that leads to a place you don't want to go?

Be well.

Chapter Three

Hard Work Doesn't Make You a Hero

Put aside the thought that you deserve a gold star for effort. What earns you kudos are results

What does it mean to genuinely work hard, and who are the two people (or rather one person and one group) you should compare yourself to?

Work is not the best place for your efforts

It still bothers me, I have to be honest, but I now see hard work doesn't make you a hero.

For much of my career, I distinguished myself (or so I thought) by working harder than most people around me.

- I worked mornings, evenings, weekends, and holidays.

- I worked when I was feeling great and when I was feeling ill.

- I worked 100-hour weeks.

Later, much later, I learned why hard work is not only insufficient for success but not the best place to invest your efforts either.

Why not? Well, there's a whole life philosophy behind the answers, which I'm sharing with you bit by bit. For today, let's say it's for two reasons:

1. The mere fact you are busy tells us nothing about the **reasons why you are busy.**

2. The quantity of work you perform says nothing in itself about the **results you deliver.**

Some people are busy because of structural inefficiencies.

- For example, their department is understaffed and they are doing the work of multiple people.

- Or their company has redundant processes, like holding weekly status update meetings and drafting memos for people who don't read them.

- Or the person themselves creates problems by letting deadlines lapse and then needing to respond to the resultant pressure in crisis mode.

This all creates stress and hard work, no doubt, but do we rank the people suffering under such structural problems as better performers because of it?

Now, consider the hard work we all sometimes do that yields no result or a negative result.

We worked like the devil but didn't complete the acquisition, win the lawsuit, or sign the contract.

We would like to be rewarded for our effort, but if we're honest, effort alone is not worth very much. In fact, the person who delivers a result with the least effort is someone we need to watch.

The obvious exception consists of people who take shortcuts in achieving their results. In business, the ends never justify the means, and a result obtained improperly is worse than a failed project.

I once had responsibility for a major initiative in an area adjacent to my core legal work. The CEO gave me the task as a chance to develop and to see how well I could perform in new areas.

And although I worked as hard on that initiative as I ever did anything, I had a string of poor performance reviews that I deserved.

Why? Because despite my admittedly hard work, we did not achieve our objectives in the timeline we wanted. My results didn't match up to my efforts.

As you advance in your career, put aside the thought that you deserve a gold star for effort. What earns you kudos are results.

The only two people you should compare yourself to

If you want to be happy in life, there is **only one comparison** you should ever make. That is, compare who you are today to who you were yesterday.

Your goal should be to make incremental progress in the direction of your choosing. If you are making steady progress in this fashion, it does not matter your pace.

Learning to compare yourself to yourself is one of the keys to a meaningful life that Stoic philosophy offers.

It allows you to be your own best judge of your performance. And if you are committed to your own improvement, the chances are excellent that you will improve your work performance as well.

Because I assume you want career success in addition to happiness, I will let you know the secret to your second comparison.

- You can greatly enhance your chance of success at work by choosing the best-performing comparison group.

- Compare yourself to the best performers *anywhere in the company*, not just among your direct peers on the legal team.

I reported to three tough graders over my in-house career. The thing that helped me most was being compared to the best performers in the whole company. These are the people driving significant value creation.

What am I doing that compares? Not in terms of perceived effort, hours worked, or even compared to other lawyers. But compared to the best that our superstars were delivering.

I had years of tough reviews as a result, but boy did I hold myself to a high standard. I developed accordingly.

Be well.

Chapter Four

Use Pragmatic Risk Management Principles to Manage Your Career

Your career ambitions come with strings attached, and you would do well to give them some explicit thought

People sometimes ask me what in-house counsel actually do. I struggled to explain it to my kids, who came away from their visits to the office with the impression that we "write emails, talk all day on the phone, and have a lot of meetings."

I also struggled to explain it to other business colleagues. In my search for a short and accurate formulation, I first came up with the words "risk mitigation." This seemed appropriate to me because we spend a great deal of time identifying risks and helping our companies avoid them or reduce the likelihood that bad things will happen.

But on deeper reflection, I realized that in-house counsel do not think of all risks equally. We have many potential risks to focus on. We exercise considerable judgment in determining where to place our limited resources.

Which topics are getting enforcement attention? Are we more exposed to some risks than others given our unique profile? Would the consequences of non-compliance be greater in this area or that one?

Our job is not to mitigate all risks

Critically, the best counsel also understand that our job is not to mitigate or eliminate all risks. We would put our companies out of business if we tried.

You can think of it this way: We are stuck in the middle of a sandwich of opposites. On the one side, we have our business partners, who are always fighting for new business. They are eager risk-takers who will always push boundaries.

The other slice of bread consists of regulators, authorities, outside counsel, and advisors. Their mission is to hold us back and stop us from potentially causing harm in the pursuit of business. They would have us eliminate risk from the business.

Managing risks is our calling

Both sides of our sandwich are made up of extremists, and left unchecked would lead to a bitter meal. We in-house counsel turn the sandwich into something delicious with the magic sauce of "risk management."

That is, we see the benefit of taking some risks, so agree in principle with our business partners about the purpose of a business. But we also see the benefit in avoiding certain other risks, so pay attention to the regulators and advisors.

"What does this have to do with career management?" I hear some of you asking.

Simply this: If you accept the premise that our value as in-house counsel lies in our effective risk management for our clients, should we not apply similar principles to managing our own careers?

Do we apply risk management to our careers?

I've had many discussions over the years with colleagues about their career ambitions. Invariably, the emphasis is on our career goals, our development, and what we want to see as the next step.

"How fast am I making progress, and is it fast enough?"

"Will this job or promotion be the best way for me to advance my career?"

"What is the best path for me to become general counsel?"

This is the business side of the sandwich talking, and I get it. My own shortlist of career advice (more on that later) includes, "Always ask for what you want."

What's missing from this calculus, however, is a realistic estimate of the costs. How well do we try to calculate what our ambitions will cost us in terms of hours of our life, time spent with family and friends, and other important priorities?

We readily advise our clients that in fact, "No, we do not want all business at any cost. We want to grow sustainably, in a compliant way, consistent with the company's values."

Growth for businesses and individuals comes at a cost

In other words, growth for both businesses and individuals involves explicit costs, compromises, and trade-offs. Your career ambitions come with strings attached, and you would do well to give them some explicit thought.

For all the talk about work-life balance, and the progress that a lot of us have made in pursuing it, greater responsibility very often comes with more hours worked and more stress.

Is hard work a necessary precondition to success? You'll have your own views on this, and I'll come back to it in a future article.

The chances are good, though, that making progress in your career will not only bring you positive things. You may be perfectly willing to pay those costs, but this requires you to be aware of what those costs will be.

For now, I want to leave you with an image and a question. Have you been managing your career like an open-faced sandwich, sitting precariously on your outstretched hand, or are you also thinking about how to manage the risks associated with your ambitions?

Be well.

Chapter Five

Don't Work From Home Yourself Out of a Job

If it is true that your job can be performed perfectly well remotely, does it necessarily follow that your job can only be performed by you?

I can't tell you how many people have told me I'm dead wrong for suggesting offices are still relevant.

"That ship has sailed," they say, or "The future of work has forever changed. I'm never going back to the office."

Indeed, at first glance, it does appear that the balance of power has shifted, with employees demanding flexibility in working arrangements and employers with no choice but to accommodate them.

I understand full well what employees are thinking. Working from home is great. Freedom, flexibility, casual dressing, and no commute. Researchers are busily collecting evidence, or at least anecdotes, about how much employee productivity is going up as a result of all the goodness.

While this is undeniably true, let me offer two thoughts for you to consider. The first is a reminder that we are hardly objective in evaluating evidence when we have a strong interest in the outcome.

Even if you trust your own thoughts, and good for you, the second item I offer for your consideration might give you pause. Namely, if it is true that your job can be performed perfectly well remotely, does it necessarily follow that your job can only be performed by you?

A case for hybrid work schedules

I came to this line of thought by asking myself why aren't we hearing more from companies themselves pushing back on the WFH phenomenon. Sure, there are a few prominent examples of companies saying they will insist all employees must return to the office, such as the big investment banks.

But most companies are either silent or have publicly embraced the idea their employees can "work from anywhere."

Before you embrace the revolution, and congratulate yourself once again for the wisdom of having avoided investment banking, have you heard what the CEOs of those banks gave as reasons for asking their employees to return to in-person work? Check out these quotes:

> *Most professionals learn their job through an apprenticeship model, which is almost impossible to replicate in the Zoom world. Over time, this drawback could dramatically undermine the character and culture.* – Jamie Dimon, JPMorgan

> *This is not ideal for us. And it's not a new normal. We know from experience that our culture of collaboration, innovation and apprenticeship thrives when our people come together, and we look forward to having more of our colleagues back in the office.* – David Solomon, Goldman Sachs

> *[The office is] where we teach, where our interns learn. That's how we develop people. Where you build all the soft cues that go with having a successful career that aren't just about Zoom presentations.* – James Gorman, Morgan Stanley

Are you confident your job does not involve any elements of collaboration, innovation, and learning? Or are these CEOs just dinosaurs who don't realize yet the world has shifted under their feet?

More worryingly, let's assume you're right: your job *can* be performed remotely.

Moreover, you work for a forward-looking company that goes to great lengths to work out the technology glitches, establish training programs for new hires, and reinforce a shared culture. Google is an example of a company that announced early its knowledge workers could work from anywhere.

If you are working in a developed market, say the United States or Europe, you are an expensive employee. Among the most expensive in the world.

Not only that, but you also may have strange ideas about the purpose of a company, and are not afraid to sue the company for the slightest perceived unequal treatment.

Tell me again what exactly makes you so desirable as an employee?

More to the point, as wonderful as you no doubt are, how much less attractive does an employee have to be who costs your company but a fraction of what you do, is grateful to have a job, and is willing to work extremely hard because they do not take their good luck for granted?

Needless to say, who is based in a country where successful lawsuits against employers are rare, and class actions do not exist.

You don't need to be overly cynical to wonder if companies are simply biding their time. Companies will learn from the pandemic-driven measures that forced home offices upon us how to make WFH efficient.

Then, as a simple, reliable, and predictable productivity measure, they will replace a percentage of the workforce every year with lower-cost employees.

After all, we've insisted that offices are irrelevant, and work can be performed from anywhere. Ironically, by pushing this issue so hard, expensive employees may be hastening their doom by inviting such an easy, direct comparison with employees globally.

Great news if you are in a developing country. Not so much if you are in Europe or the United States.

Be well.

PS — Don't be too depressed with the possibility that WFH will make you uncompetitive and therefore redundant.

Turns out that it's not just the investment banks who realized face-to-face collaboration is kind of important. They were just the first ones courageous enough to say it.

In September 2021 Google itself announced it was paying US$2.1 billion to buy a Manhattan office building. "Wait, what? Is the WFH champion adding office space? Whatever for?" Google's comment accompanying the purchase speaks volumes:

> *We know that our employees, in order to be really happy and productive, need to collaborate. Because of that need to collaborate, we've been investing more and more in office space.*

Chapter Six

How To Implement a Project With Lackluster Management Support

Here's how to implement a project without the CEO being a cheerleader

I have read a lot of advice over my career.

There is a steady stream of new and existing rules that companies are expected to comply with or face sometimes terrible consequences.

This environment creates uncertainty and fear, which in turn creates business opportunities for a lot of people.

Consultants and law firms and "subject matter experts" of all kinds emerge to offer their services in helping you understand new rules and implement projects to ensure you stay compliant. Compliance, in other words, is big business.

As a result, I am used to hearing people pitch how to implement the latest requirement, best practice, or trending idea.

And there is one element to many pitches that demonstrates well that supposed experts don't work in the same world as you and me.

I refer, of course, to the dreaded requirement to ensure you have "top management support."

I get it. Of course, it would be easier to push through your latest project if you had the unanimous backing of the board of directors, the CEO, and the executive committee.

Looking back over the years, how many times has your project honestly warranted, let alone actually received, that kind of support?

I can think of a few instances where the stars were so aligned. Usually, yours is one of hundreds of projects, all important in their own right. Why should yours be singled out as one of the *most important*?

Telling a hapless manager that ensuring top management support is a critical success factor for their project is more than unhelpful. It's a bit like saying, "OK, first ensure an unlimited source of reliable, cheap, clean, renewable energy..."

I want to know how to implement a project without the CEO being a cheerleader. I want a consultant who can tell me how to get attention among hundreds of competing projects and priorities.

As a civic service for everyone who has been there, here is a checklist for how to implement a project with lackluster management support.

1. Gain some perspective about your project

Accept that your project is one of many and get a realistic sense of your project's relative importance — not to you, but to your company. This requires you to understand what other important initiatives your company is working on, and why.

2. Stay humble about your role

Remember that gaining this perspective is not about you, and not about your CEO or management team. You are hard-working and rightly focused on your area of responsibility. Your CEO is almost certainly hard-working as well and dealing with a tremendous complexity of topics.

Virtually every proposal the CEO evaluates come with an assertive manager saying "This is the most important project. We have to drop everything and do it now!" All your CEO learns from such a pitch is that the manager doesn't have a good sense of the broader picture.

3. Know what's hot at your company

Identify the initiatives that currently **do have** top management support. Who is championing them, who is working on them, what is the timeline, what are some upcoming deliverables, etc.? Become knowledgeable about what strategic imperatives your company is working on and why.

4. Find a link between your project and that hot ticket

Evaluate whether there are any areas of overlap between a current strategic priority and your new project. Your link may be direct, it may be tenuous. There is always a link. It's your job to find that link.

5. Identify a partner in arms

Once you've found one or more links, find out who is currently working on the strategic priority that may be affected by your link. This person could be at any level in the organization and is typically not among the senior-most managers involved.

Your target is more likely either responsible for seeing a part of the project implemented, or would be directly affected by a potential delay, failure, or problem if an unforeseen risk was missed.

6. Design your pitch to solve your partner's problem

Sure, your partner was unaware a problem existed until you brought it to their attention. Yes, the problem is actually a result of the new rule or regulation you are trying to comply with. But you are not the problem.

You are the person saving your partner from an embarrassing omission. Not because you point out the problem. That will just get you killed as the messenger of bad news. But because you point out the problem and come with a ready-made solution.

7. Be prepared to implement your solution without help

Perfect compliance is not the goal at this stage. You want to start small, with something that you can do and do correctly and well. Your partner needs to understand that you are not asking for anything but to spend **your own** valuable time and effort on helping solve **their** problem.

8. Meet others on the main project

Once you are officially working on the main strategic priority, even though it is in your narrow area of interest, ask your partner to involve you in broader meetings. If you have been constructive and helpful, not asked for any resources, and not caused any new problems, you should be OK.

9. Gently spread your idea

This should be mainly through awareness raising amongst others working on the project: For example, that the issue is out there, that it has real-world consequences, and that you are working on a solution to a narrow piece of it.

Your goal is to get people in other areas of responsibility to acknowledge the issue in their own presentations. If you are very lucky, some of them will look into the topic on their own and may identify additional risks/opportunities for further implementation.

10. Ride the wave

Either your issue has real-world relevance, or it does not. If the issue is relevant, then you will have:

- Put yourself in a position to bring it to the attention of relevant people who are in a position to do something about it;

- Shown yourself to be selfless and helpful, a good team member; and

- Demonstrated yourself as a subject-matter expert with knowledge about the issue.

If your issue is not yet ripe or has been over-exaggerated by the expert class promoting consulting services, or your company is not yet ready, etc., you will still have made a good first step and laid the foundation for future steps when circumstances change.

Or, if all this sounds too time-consuming or Machiavellian, by all means, pitch your project directly to the CEO.

I recommend telling your CEO that yours is the most important project in the world, and that the company has to drop everything to implement it immediately. Let me know how it goes.

Be well.

Chapter Seven

With Experience Comes ... Patience

Adjusting your priorities to suit a colleague's laziness or incompetence only enables them and harms you

We normally assume it is wisdom that comes from experience. No doubt this is true for some of us.

But I wonder if what we think of as wisdom is based on a healthy foundation of patience.

Let me give you one small example to illustrate the idea.

Have any of you ever been away from work and neglected to respond to an URGENT request, only to find the matter resolved upon your return?

If you have ever managed to step entirely away from your work for a week or more, I expect you've experienced this.

What can we learn from this phenomenon?

Well, it could be that people are incautious in their requests, and label them "URGENT" when they are not urgent. Or perhaps, for matters that are truly urgent, the requestor finds another way to satisfy their request when they realize you are absent.

Either scenario might lead you to ask yourself, "Why did they come to me in the first instance when there was another way for them to get what they needed?"

Requests within the scope of your job

Maybe the request falls clearly within the scope of your job. Then I think we would agree it is reasonable for people to ask you for help.

- Most of us are not bothered by legitimate requests, so long as they are legitimately delivered.

- A legitimate request becomes an inappropriate burden to us when the person simply sits on it for no good reason other than poor time management.

We've all experienced a request for expedited service only to realize our counterpart could have asked for our help weeks earlier.

I don't know about you, but it burns me up to respond in crisis mode when an issue has become a burning issue because of someone else's negligence.

The Chairman of my company asked us to follow two simple rules when making requests of others. I try hard to honor these rules in all cases:

1. Always assume the person you are approaching is **as busy as you are**. They are not sitting idle waiting for your request. Your proposed deadline must take the recipient's busy schedule into account.

2. After considering the first point, **tailor your proposed deadline** to the difficulty of the task. You should propose a shorter deadline for responses that take only a moment to deliver. But allow more time for tasks that take more time.

You might find these rules blindingly obvious and simple. I do, too.

But ask yourself how often people observe the rules in practice, and you will appreciate the beauty of learning to follow them yourself.

Requests outside the scope of your job

So far I've been talking about legitimate requests, i.e., those on topics within the scope of our jobs. How shall we think about requests that fall outside the scope of our jobs?

For all the things that we **must** do, there is a great number that we **could** do. And because we are conscientious, hard-working, and competent, in our heart of hearts we know we can do many things better than our work colleagues themselves.

Have you ever found yourself doing something that was technically a co-worker's job?

- Maybe they asked you nicely and you didn't want to say no.

- Maybe you knew you could do it relatively quickly and it would save you time later not to have to correct their sloppy work.

Whatever your rationale, consider that you may be sabotaging your own success.

If you have any meaningful responsibilities, then you are already busy. If you are working strategically, then you have already set your own priorities.

Yes, we adjust our priorities according to external circumstances. But adjusting your priorities to suit a colleague's laziness or incompetence only enables them and harms you.

Now I suspect you are more tactful than I am and would never call your colleagues lazy or incompetent, at least not to their faces. This is where patience masquerading as wisdom comes to your rescue.

No matter what type of URGENT requests you receive, simply continue to do your own work according to your own priorities.

- The person who is trying to get you to do their work for them will see that you do not rise to the bait. They will eventually look elsewhere with no drama.

- The person who has mismanaged their time needs to suffer consequences for their failure. Let them. Even if this means they try to escalate to your boss. If they have caused a crisis for you by their own poor time management, your boss will also see it.

- And if an unexpected, truly urgent topic comes up that deserves your immediate attention according to your pre-determined strategy and priorities, you may work on it with a clean conscience. But only then.

So in sum: Stick to your own priorities.

No need for an ugly confrontation. No need for bitterness. Only patience. Maybe that's true wisdom after all.

Be well.

Chapter Eight

Do You Know Your Gear Ratio?

Past a noticeable point, more effort makes things worse, not better

O ne of the best things I did to improve the *quality* of my work was to decrease the *quantity* of it.

I don't know why it took me so long to figure out that simply working more hours was not the only or best path to better performance.

You'd think I'd have learned this lesson in my first associate job after putting in 100-hour weeks and pulling regular all-nighters. There comes a point when just grinding out more hours definitely becomes counter-productive.

If you've tried writing a coherent sentence after working for 36 hours straight, you'll know what I mean.

Exercise re-energizes and reduces stress

But I didn't learn the lesson for almost ten years. I let myself get overweight and sedentary, avoiding any kind of physical exercise until my 30s.

But after an epiphany one day (I'll tell you about it sometime if you're interested), I looked to my fitness with a passion.

- I was prepared to accept sacrifices in my work by devoting time each day to my health.

- To my surprise and delight, substituting work time for exercise time made all my remaining time that much more productive.

Exercise is beneficial for so many reasons. When I mentor and coach newly promoted managers, the first and best advice I share with them is to develop an exercise habit if they don't already exercise regularly.

In my particular overworked case, exercising reset my stress levels and allowed me to return to work feeling relaxed and ready.

The Yerkes-Dodson Law

Perhaps you've heard of the Yerkes-Dodson Law, deriving from research the pair of psychologists published in the early 1900s.

When undertaking challenging mental tasks, which I think describes a lot of legal work, performance increases with mental arousal up to a point, after which it decreases.

Visualize a bell curve showing performance increasing as stress increases but then dropping off as the stress continues to go up.

Gear ratio

Let's consider Yerkes-Dodson as it applies to exercise. Perhaps because I started working out at a more mature age, I was definitely a nerd about my exercise.

I loved the gear and gadgets (and still do), such as functional clothing, heart rate monitors, and GPS trackers. Tracking workouts and seeing what insights I could tease out of the data was sometimes as satisfying as the workout itself.

In automotive terms, a gear ratio refers to the number of rotations a driver gear makes to the gear being driven. For each rotation of a 28-tooth gear, for example, a 7-tooth gear must rotate four times, expressed as 4:1.

We can think of our gear ratio in terms of our personal performance. First our physical performance, then our mental performance.

I started out by running, and eventually experimented with triathlons (swimming, biking, and running), before adding hiking to the mix.

- My tracking data showed I have a reasonably consistent 2:1 gear ratio.

- That is, I bike twice as fast as I run, I run twice as fast as I hike, and I hike twice as fast as I swim.

This says absolutely nothing about whether I'm fast or slow. In fact, I'm pretty average, despite lots of practice.

What the ratio tells me is there is a level of effort at which I am most efficient in each sporting discipline. If I push my speed (or effort) too far beyond what I'm geared for, I run the risk of burning out much more quickly.

Past a noticeable point, more effort makes things worse, not better.

Anyone who's started out too quickly in a race has learned this the hard way. I must be a slow learner, for I am still prone to overestimating my capabilities on race day.

Know your high and low points as you schedule your day

So it is with work. In the work setting, your gear ratio will refer to things like the following:

- What time of day are you sharpest? Are the morning hours your friend, or are you at home among the night owls?

- How long can you profitably work before you take a break? Most people find something between one and two hours ideal.

- What types of work do you most enjoy, for example, writing, talking, thinking, etc.?

- What sorts of situations stress you out and drain your tank the quickest? Do you thrive or shy away from negotiations, public speaking, terminations, investigations, and so on?

Your particular variables will differ and you will probably be geared differently than your colleagues and me.

My advice for you: Spend some quality time thinking about how you're geared. You can then mindfully leverage your strengths to ensure you work most effectively.

Taking a break and switching gears is sometimes the best way to improve your performance.

Be well.

Chapter Nine

Can You Be Too Good at Your Job?

Your colleagues will, by inaction, invite you to do some of their work on top of the load you are already carrying

"Too good at your job," you wonder. "Is that even a thing?"

Believe it or not, there are ways in which stellar performance may create some unintended consequences. You can decide for yourself whether the benefits of being a super-employee are worth the potential risks.

The reason for your initial skepticism is that most employees are far from being too good at their jobs. Many colleagues show up, do their work (sort of), and scurry off.

I hear far more complaints from in-house friends about their needing to work extra hard to compensate for others' inefficiencies and thoughtlessness than that they are overcome with awesomeness.

This post is about you, though, not your sometimes suboptimal colleagues. You didn't get to where you are today by being a slacker.

The habits you learned in school and earlier serve you well in the workplace.

- You prepare, show up early, work hard, and pay attention.

- You observe your behavior and that of others around you so that you may more successfully navigate the sometimes turbulent currents of your company's culture.

You don't have a choice but to learn to work well because you're too busy to waste time on lower-priority tasks. You hone your skills every day by necessity.

As a result, like you, many in-house counsel are superb at their jobs. Because of their broad exposure to all corners of their companies' businesses, their analytical approach, and their ruthless prioritization of strategic tasks, in-house counsel are among the best employees overall.

I used to tell my team my goal was for the business to "cherish" in-house counsel. That is, when there was a vacancy, the business should be delighted with the opportunity to add another lawyer to the team because of how greatly we added value to the company in every opportunity that presented itself.

Competence attracts new work like bees to pollen

What are some consequences of being great at your job? Well, one obvious consequence that will no doubt have occurred to you is that competence attracts new work like bees to pollen.

To whom do you assign important projects as a manager? The employee who has free time but a spotty track record or the superstar who crushes everything you throw at them?

Work is not at all evenly or fairly distributed because managers are selfish. We want the best person for the job even though that person is already doing twice as much as their colleagues.

I call this the "curse of competence." People who are busy because they are good at their jobs will receive a disproportionate amount of additional work.

Colleagues sometimes take advantage of high-performing team members

And it's not just bosses who notice this. Your colleagues notice your work performance as well. Most will greatly appreciate all that you do.

A certain subset, however, will take advantage of your desire to outperform by being just a little bit more incompetent.

Say you are on a project together and a summary of a meeting needs to be drafted, or some work product needs to be created for the project to advance. Your opportunistic free rider just sits back and lets the pressure build, even if they've been assigned part of the work.

They care more about managing their time than they do advancing the project. You care more about doing a good job and before long you feel compelled to step into the gap.

Result? Your colleagues will, by inaction, invite you to do some of their work on top of the load you are already carrying.

This leads to a spiral of overwork that has led many great performers to burn out. While some enlightened managers look for this and will help protect their stars, you simply can't count on it.

Do you really need to move from twice as productive to three times?

If you recall that your goal is not short-term overperformance but long-term sustainable performance, it may be easier for you to take steps to protect yourself.

You're already twice as productive as others. Do you really need to be three times as productive?

Find a pace you can sustain and stick to it

How do you protect yourself from the perils of being too good at your job? By finding a pace of work that you can sustain and sticking to it.

No one who appreciates their fine car would push the engine past the redline for extended periods. What makes you think pushing yourself beyond your comfort zone at work is any better for you?

Work deliberately and steadily, take breaks when you need to, and stop when you've put in a full day.

No matter how much you have to do, no matter how much additional work your colleagues try to pile on, work on the most important priority first and take the time needed to do a good job.

You are not slowing down as much as you are working well at a manageable pace.

If you do this, you will notice good things start to happen. Your boss will see your response time is no longer immediate, even though you're still producing first-rate work on everything you do. If they're in a hurry, they will start to look elsewhere.

When you fail to do your colleagues' work for them, they will either fail themselves (sad, but not your problem) or, more frequently, they will rediscover their own capacity for work.

In other words, people will pick up on how you work and they will adjust themselves to your work habits.

Thus, I recommend you continue to maintain high standards for everything you do, but find ways to not do everything you may be asked to do.

I trust you'll find your business still cherishes you just as much.

Be well.

Chapter Ten

What Would You Do With 1OOO Hours?

Regardless of external rewards or pressure, it is eminently valuable to determine for ourselves how best to invest our time

This article is not about sports, even though it might seem like it. This article is also not about personal fitness, although you could be forgiven for thinking so.

Today's article is about making use of our second most precious commodity, after our well-reasoned minds: time. As such, even if you could give a fig for swimming, biking, or running, I urge you to stay the course with me today. The reward for reaching the finish line may be a lesson that brings you far in life.

What does 1000 hours represent?

- It's a bit more than 11 percent of all the hours in a year. If you subtract out, say, eight hours a night for sleep, and time spent working a full-time job, that still leaves us with something like 4000 hours at our annual disposal.

- If you make US$10/hour, working 1000 hours gets you a bit less than US$9000 after tax. If you're a lawyer charging US$500 an hour, you'll gross a cool half a million, although you'll pay a lot in taxes.

- The World Health Organization recommends we all get at least 150 minutes of exercise a week, or 2 1/2 hours. At that rate, you'd need almost eight years to hit your 1000 hours. We can be more ambitious. Most fit people I know invest an hour a day on average in their training, say 400 hours a year. For them, 1000 hours is 2 1/2 years of training.

The 1000 hours that have been weighing on my mind

Why do I raise all this? I've been grappling with a decision for some time. *Should I commit to doing an* Ironman? This is the ultimate of triathlons, comprising a 3.9-kilometer swim, 180-kilometer bike ride, and then running 42.2 kilometers, a full marathon.

Although a handful of the world's fittest can complete this distance in under eight hours, non-elite times cluster around 12 hours. The course cutoff is usually 17 hours.

As impressive as this feat may be, the training to be able to show up on race day dwarfs the race itself. And it is the training for an Ironman more than the event itself that has been giving me pause.

The absolute best thing about having fit friends is that they inspire you to be more fit. The absolute worst thing about having fit friends is that they sometimes inspire you to crazy fitness goals.

I expect that most often I've been the one encouraging friends and colleagues to bake regular fitness into their lives.

With an annual marathon streak extending over 20 years, I wanted to demonstrate with my actions that a regular fitness habit could coexist with a demanding management job. Although the marathons themselves were stressful, the knowledge that one was coming up gave me motivation to be consistent in my training.

It doesn't help that I've had an Ironman on my secret bucket list for a long time. In my case, I would need to build up my basic bike endurance before I could even start race training. Realistically, to perform as I'd like in a race, I would need to devote 10–15 hours a week to my training for the next year and a half. Hence the 1000-hour question.

Why do we want to do what we want to do?

Having done all this preparation and thinking, I find myself asking a Stoic question. What would I be doing the Ironman race for?

Is it for bragging rights (yes) or to check an item off a decades-old list (yes)? Is it to show camaraderie and have some fun with friends (yes and yes)? Is it to maintain or gain fitness? Hmmm.

I cannot in good faith dispense Stoic advice without admitting that most of these potential rationales don't stand up to deep scrutiny.

I want to stay fit and healthy and avoid injury. Nothing about biking six straight hours is necessary for that. If I'm honest, I suspect little about running marathons is necessary for long-term health and avoiding injury either.

At the same time, I've really enjoyed my new workouts: swimming, biking, yoga, and even strength training.

What do we value most highly?

If I was following my own advice, I would say look to the underlying value of things. What is it we *really want* to accomplish? What will we be most happy about looking back in a couple of years?

No doubt I would be gratified to have that Ironman medal and the accompanying backpack and t-shirt, etc. I would look back on the accomplishment with pride for a long time.

The wise thing to do might be to take the same hours I'd be willing to commit to Ironman training and devote them to a sensible mix of fitness-focused workouts. Do them all in such frequencies and amounts that keep them fun for the long term. Will someone give me a medal for this? Probably not.

Then again, I am reminded of what I learned about the danger of being too easy on ourselves when faced with challenges. We become stronger by embracing challenges. Thus, there is great value in pursuing outrageous and even scary goals.

This thought process is no different than deciding what is the most valuable use of our time at work.

Regardless of external rewards or pressure, it is eminently valuable to determine for ourselves how best to invest our time. In fact, it is the most valuable thing we can do, if we can follow the conclusions our thinking leads us to.

Each year, we've got 4000 hours of free time at our disposal. How about we make a conscious choice to direct just 25 percent of that time?

What will you do with 1000 hours?

Be well.

PS — I let my fears gain the upper hand last year. No more. I am not sure how or when, but an Ironman is in my future.

Chapter Eleven

Your Attitude Is the Best Predictor of Success

A person with average abilities but a superior attitude will outperform a person with great abilities and a poor attitude

We usually think it is our abilities that determine what we can achieve. While our abilities are no doubt relevant, I've come to believe they are not determinant.

The reason is that if you want something badly enough, you will find a way to make it happen. You will gather to yourself new abilities, find new paths to achieve your objectives, and enlist others to your cause.

What do experienced managers look for when hiring?

I was running with a friend recently. Among other things, he spent years working in human resources. We were talking about our experiences hiring new employees.

I said I felt a person's attitude was the most important criterion in making a good hire. Far more important than their school, where they worked previously, or what projects they worked on. Most of that tells me little about how they'll perform their new tasks in this new setting.

A person with average abilities but a superior attitude will outperform a person with great abilities and a poor attitude. And I know which one I want on my team because I see how they perform in practice.

What is a superior attitude?

Because it's important to understand the point, let me elaborate on what I mean by a superior attitude. A person with a superior attitude is humble, enthusiastic, and optimistic.

- They know they don't know everything they need to and that they can't yet do everything they'll be asked to do.

- But they are open to trying new, hard things and figuring out along the way how to do them well.

- Their optimism is reflected in their volunteering for new projects and their response to challenges.

- When inevitable setbacks arise, they are not thrown off course or out of balance.

- They rise to the challenge and find a way to overcome it. This attitude makes all the difference between giving up and pushing through to success.

A person with a superior attitude doesn't make excuses for their performance. When they mess up, they acknowledge it. More importantly, you can see they are motivated to learn from their mistakes and not repeat them.

They certainly don't blame others for what happens to them. Even when external circumstances play a role, they focus on what they can control and don't waste time in worrying about what they cannot.

Attitude helps on the journey

I came across a person with an amazingly superior attitude and willingness to put in the hard work necessary for success.

This is Nims Purja, the celebrated Nepali climber who smashed several mountaineering world records, after serving with the British Armed Forces as a Nepalese Gurkha and a soldier in the Special Boat Service (SBS) elite special forces unit of the Royal Navy.

He describes what he did in the recent book Beyond Possible: One Man, 14 Peaks, and the Mountaineering Achievement of a Lifetime. Although his physical feats defy many people's comprehension, I was struck most by Nim's descriptions of his attitude along his journey.

He set out on a mission to climb all 14 of the world's 8,000-meter peaks in a record time: Less than seven months, compared to the prior record of seven *years* and 10 months. Why? He says he wanted to "prove to the world that everything, *anything*, was possible if you dedicated your heart and mind to a plan."

Over and over, he talks about his attitude as being the single most important factor in his success.

He repeatedly dealt with skepticism, doubt, and negative emotions by shrugging them off and by reframing each situation to find something positive:

From an early age, I believed in the power of positive thinking and willed myself through illnesses and chronic ailments.

I believed.... It surrounded me like a force field and I soon learned that with relentless self-belief, anything was possible.

Getting angry about the situation wasn't going to help ... remaining emotionally strong was imperative: Flipping a negative event into positive momentum was the only way to remain focused on my primary objective.

I attacked everything with positive thinking.

I never moaned when the going got tough. Instead, I ... led by example, maintaining team morale through hard effort and positive thinking. —Nims Purja

There are many more statements like this, but you get the point — It is Nims's indomitable will, as much as his physical abilities, that got him through his many challenges.

How to cultivate an indomitable attitude

Our challenges may not be matters of life and death as when summiting 8,000-meter peaks. But the attitudes we bring to our challenges may be just as determinative of our success.

- Tell yourself you are up to the challenges you face and that you will do everything necessary to succeed.

- Tell yourself that you will not only deal with adversity but welcome the unexpected troubles that are sure to arise. You will think of a way to find the positive in every situation.

- Tell yourself you will be stronger, happier, and better by virtue of all that you do.

If you keep telling yourself these things, chances are good others will be telling the stories of your amazing accomplishments for you.

Be well.

Chapter Twelve

Share Your Secret Plans

One great way to make your plans come true is by sharing them with someone who cares for you

H as this ever happened to you? You wrestle in silence with the thought of seeking a promotion, moving house, or changing a relationship.

When you finally get to the point of airing and sharing your thoughts with a friend, you find out they have been grappling with many of the same questions.

My wife and I have concluded everyone is entertaining what we call "secret plans," *all the time*. Maybe it's a form of escapism, maybe it's just daydreaming.

We have found it does not matter how grounded or stable or established someone is, chances are, they are secretly planning something.

The green grass over there

Let's face it. We all know the grass is greener over there, so why shouldn't we be thinking about moseying on over? Progress requires change, and because we all want to progress, doesn't that mean we have to contemplate change?

There is nothing particularly profound about this. I think the point is that we should not think we are alone in our worries, our wants, and our cares. Everyone is trying to figure out the right thing to do, and no one is certain they have figured it out.

One great way to make your plans come true is by sharing them with someone who cares for you. Discuss your desires, evaluate alternatives.

Just by saying out loud what you want, you acknowledge your wishes to yourself. By speaking your thoughts to another, you help yourself figure out more clearly what you are after.

If you can describe something so that someone else understands it, you improve your own understanding of it. Finally, the chances are good your friend will be a better sounding board to you than you can be to yourself, at least on some points.

This approach can work well in your career development. We have so many thoughts and ideas and sometimes conflicting emotions. Find a few trusted confidants you can talk to about what's on your mind.

You may get good input. You will certainly think more deeply about what it is you are trying to achieve in the process of describing it to someone else.

Tell your boss — Yes, really

I will go further and say that you should discuss your ambitions with your boss and with management.

Do you think you are the only employee who has grappled with career decisions? Almost certainly your boss has, and almost certainly, several of your colleagues are thinking about similar topics right now.

Don't you think your boss would prefer to know what's on your mind? Even if, no, *especially if* one of the things you are contemplating is leaving for another job?

"Well, yes," you may be thinking. "I am sure my boss *would* like to know what's on my mind. But if I tell her I'm thinking about jumping ship, that will ruin our working relationship in the event I don't leave."

I understand you, and I agree some bosses behave badly in these situations. But a good boss will welcome the chance to discuss this with you.

You may find that boss already knows (or suspects) you are looking. You may find your boss has some alternatives to offer you for consideration. You may also find your relationship with your boss is ultimately improved by virtue of the trust you showed in sharing your thoughts.

I know you will be hesitant to talk to your boss about your secret plans.

I urge you to consider whether this is because you believe you have a bad boss who will punish you (in which case you have other, fruitful boss-management topics to pursue), or because you are afraid of what might happen.

In the meantime, you could first find a friend or colleague with whom you can confidentially discuss your thoughts.

Either way, you may find you can move your secret plans closer to reality by sharing the secret.

Be well.

Chapter Thirteen

If You Want To Get Ahead, Go Back to the Office

It's never been easier to stand out at work. One of the best ways is simple: Go to the office

Search for "*Work from home is here to stay*" and you will find many articles confirming it is so. Everyone is happy to tell you that work has changed forever.

The fact that this is what people very much want to believe is irrelevant. For the foreseeable future, many of us who wish to work from home will be able to do so. And most of us will be as productive as we were before if not more so.

If you are interested in advancing your career, however, there has never been a better time to go back to the office.

Rarely are we given so clear a chance to gain a competitive advantage over our peers. And relatively simply at that. Usually, it takes solid, substantive performance over the long term to have such good prospects of getting ahead.

Consider this your golden opportunity.

Why? Here are three good reasons: Management is there, your colleagues are not, and you will have many opportunities to stand out.

Your boss still goes to the office

Some number of people will continue going to the office regularly. Senior management is among them. There are multiple reasons for this.

Important people with significant responsibilities often have offices and support staff. Some have a whole ecosystem to help them be productive at work.

Yes, during the pandemic a certain number of managers worked from home. Most have long since returned to the office. Having an office at work, and needing to be in that office, are new status symbols in the work-from-home era. It is how managers show they are important.

Your colleagues are staying at home

Working from home is great! We all know it, so we want to keep doing it. Smart people worked out the technology for anyone to work anywhere. We can get up when we want, wear what we want, and take breaks when we want.

Much of the day was wasted in the office anyway. By working in focused blocks at home, we can be incredibly productive and get the same work done in less time.

And best of all, the pandemic made it necessary for a lot of us. Employees were glad to push the scales back in favor of the individual in the work-life balance. Companies simply could not say no.

Thus, it's easy to predict that many, many people will continue working from home and there's little companies can do about it. Although there's one obvious response CFOs will likely pursue:

It's a great time to shine

Standing out in a crowd is hard. Standing out among only a handful of people is something else entirely. The casual encounter in the hallway is anything but. The invitation to join the boss for a coffee break or a snack is your opportunity.

"But," you say, "when there are fewer people around, you are at greater risk of getting assigned more work."

That's exactly the point, you see. Bosses love employees who volunteer to take on projects. We're just trying to get the work done without drama or stress.

A team member who is always cheerful, who helps out often, and who isn't needy is a treasure. We will work hard to keep such an employee happy and productive.

So your bosses will be in the office. Not too many other people will be. Who comes in and what they do there will make all the difference to some careers.

What to do when you are in the office

For all the talk about overcoming implicit bias and unconscious bias, people seem to have forgotten how powerful it is. We like people who are like us. That means people who do similar things, have similar interests, and hold similar values.

When you see a colleague in the hallway and exchange a few words about a non-work topic, you have many opportunities to make a connection. Listen carefully and you can find out about their interests. Respond thoughtfully and you can reveal shared interests.

Do not eat at your desk in some vain thought of being productive. It is not a waste of time to have lunch with colleagues. I can't tell you how many key business initiatives were launched by a simple ask at a casual lunch following a relaxed, shared rapport.

Fairness has nothing to do with it

Is any of this fair to your colleagues who are working from home? I don't think so.

Should you be worried about it? That's a personal choice you have to make. I would just say that the world is filled with asymmetries of circumstances. Rather than bemoaning the world's unfairness, you could leverage strategies that work to your advantage.

The world is competitive. If you want to outperform, be prepared to work hard and take every advantage on offer.

- Show up early, stay late, and volunteer to do projects no one else wants.

- Always do your best and stay positive, especially when you are doing thankless tasks.

Trust me, you will stand out, now more than ever, when most people are focused on optimizing their work to suit their private lives.

Be well.

IMPORTANT CAVEAT: Many of your colleagues will have a more relaxed life than you. They will work less for the same pay, and they will have less stress. They will be that much closer to a healthy work-life balance.

Chapter Fourteen

Are You Globally Competitive in Your Career?

These questions will help you objectively benchmark yourself against your peers

D o you know if your company considers you a valuable employee? How do you compare to other employees, not just where you happen to be working right now, but across the globe?

These questions will help you objectively benchmark yourself. If you answer five or fewer of the following questions with "Yes," then you may not be as competitive globally as you think.

1. Are you relentlessly positive?

Can you find something to be happy about every day when you start work? Do you bring a smile to your face when you encounter colleagues in the hallway? Can you find a kind word for a co-worker who is struggling? Can you be forgiving when someone has frustrated your plans, and is being stubborn and unhelpful?

Not to be corny, but do you break into a spontaneous whistle or song because you enjoy what you're doing?

Or are you the person who can always be found complaining around the water cooler? Every business commits countless follies, after all. If we're honest, not a day goes by without some idiot doing something to annoy us. What's the harm in pointing these things out? After all, how else will things get better?

2. Can you be counted on to volunteer for projects?

Are you the first one to raise your hand when management proposes a new project? Do you pitch in to help even when the project is outside your area of expertise? Do you volunteer for projects despite being genuinely busy with your own work? Do you even volunteer to work on tasks that are important, but unglamorous?

Or do you refuse to volunteer for more work because you're focused on your own priorities? Do you prefer to stay in your area of expertise? Do you carefully avoid doing work that is repetitive, boring, or thankless?

3. Are you (relatively) inexpensive?

Are there any employees where you work who are paid more than you for the same or similar work? Are there employees *anywhere in the world* who are paid more than you for the same or similar work? If you look at broad-based market surveys, are you at or around the median salary?

Or are you comfortable being paid more than anyone else? Because after all, you worked hard and you deserve it. And even if your salary is relatively high, you have to look out for yourself, because no one else will do it.

4. Do you spend at least an hour each day working on your strategic priorities?

This means topics that *you* have identified as the most important and most valuable. These will vary frequently depending on what is going on in your business and in your team. The key factor is that you make it happen every day (or as near to it as possible) to spend at least some time on your self-identified priorities.

Or do you spend your days busy? Busy with meetings and calls, administration and personnel issues, responding to emails, and putting out urgent fires.

5. Do you manage your physical fitness like you would a vital project at work?

One way to tell if you should answer yes is if you have a daily or weekly physical fitness habit. Do you walk or bike to work? Do you shun elevators and walk up and down all the stairs you can find? Do you join friends for a weekly yoga or dance class?

There is no end of choices. The key is, do you treat your physical fitness as one of your most important strategic priorities?

Or do you find yourself skipping a workout because of an urgent project at work? Do you find yourself sleeping in when you had planned to exercise because you've been so busy that "you deserve time off"?

6. Do you set aside at least one day a month for strategic thinking and planning?

This could also be a few hours each week, or half a day every two weeks. The point is, do you invest regularly in quality blocks of time where you are thinking strategically and updating your plans?

Or do you feel satisfied with accomplishing tasks and getting things done? You are too busy to take 10% of your time to just sit and think.

7. Are you a woman or a minority?

This is just a yes-no question. I am not putting any judgment or criticism behind it.

I've been in many search discussions, across public companies, private companies, for-profits, and charitable enterprises. In 30 years, I have never once heard the phrase, "We need to fill this role with a white guy."

I have, however, heard every variation of the phrase "We need to fill this role with _____ (every other variation)."

8. Do you expose yourself to new ideas regularly?

I originally wrote "Do you read widely for business and pleasure, and learn something new every week?" In the meantime, there are more options than just reading, including podcasts, audiobooks, online courses, and more.

The point is whether you are constantly seeking to learn new things and to be exposed to unfamiliar ideas.

Or do you feel that your school days are behind you and thank goodness. That books are painfully boring, and if they can't get the point across in a 30-second TikTok video, what's the point?

9. Are you OK with your salary?

No matter how much you are paid, do you trust your company to pay you fairly, based on broad-based market comparisons? Do you believe that the reward for work is measured in more than money? For example, in things like your professional development, having colleagues you like and respect, and in working for a company that has values aligned with your own?

Or do you regularly check the salary surveys to see if others are making more than you, and bring these surveys to the attention of your boss? Do you secretly worry that you are not being paid the same as others doing the same work? Does it bother you to know friends who are making lots more money than you?

10. Can you describe your strategy and key priorities in sixty seconds?

In other words, do you effectively build a common understanding of your value proposition? We all have countless competing demands for time and resources.

Does your team understand what the vision is and why what they are working on is important? Do your colleagues understand what you do and why? Does management understand how you are making a vital contribution?

Yes, I am referring to the elevator speech.

Or when someone asks you what's keeping you busy, do you make the mistake of simply describing the details of what you're working on at the moment?

Bonus question: Would you call yourself happy?

This is of course related to the first question. Being positive is a good way to become happy. Happiness is a condition that can be cultivated, often through simple steps that you can take regularly.

Your career can certainly make you happy, but too often people make themselves miserable in pursuit of their ambitions. It is my sincere desire to help on both the career front and the happiness front.

I hope this has been helpful to you in thinking about your competitiveness at work.

Be well.

Chapter Fifteen

It's TIME WE JOG

This is a simple slogan to organize factors that will contribute to your personal and professional success

T hose who know me will realize it is a complete coincidence that these factors sum up as a reminder to be physically fit. Here they are:

T — Trust

Be trustworthy and reliable. People will want to work with you and will give you more opportunities if they trust you and if you deliver reliably.

I — Integrity

When evaluating a company, the integrity and ethics of management are vital. You shall reinforce the importance of integrity with your own behavior.

M — Motivation

Understand what motivates you, so that you can apply those levers to your work and your life. You will have to motivate yourself often, so know how to do it effectively.

Once you have decided on goals, be persistent, push, and never give up.

E — Example

Always set an example with your personal behavior of what you expect others to do. Be a role model, on both personal and professional topics.

W — Work-life balance

Performing at an elevated level sustainably requires you to acknowledge the different priorities in your life: not just work, but also family, health, community, society, etc.

You will not achieve a work-life balance by accident, so plan to spend time on it often.

E — Emotional intelligence

To perform at a high level, you need self-awareness and emotional intelligence, which includes knowing how you interact with others. Ask for feedback and take it seriously but not personally.

If you can, cultivate a positive mindset. Not only will you be happier, but people like being around optimistic people, which generates opportunities for you.

J — Judgment

This is the most important professional attribute for any knowledge worker because you must constantly balance risk management with pragmatism. Your value comes from your judgment on what risks it is appropriate to take, and in setting priorities.

O — Opportunities

Make sure to ask for what you want. At the same time, be open to opportunities to do more, to do different things. Your big break may come in an unexpected area, so take a chance, and volunteer.

Trust that you will be able to add value to new areas. This is what helps you grow.

G — Good job

Do a good job in your current job. This is a reality check against the prior point. No matter how keenly you want the next step in your career, you will never get there if your performance in your current job is lacking.

Have dreams for the future but focus on what you are doing right now.

Nothing helps you do a good job so much as following continuous improvement principles. Just start with where you are and steadily improve.

Be well.

Chapter Sixteen

These Things May Be Hurting Your Career

This list helps you check whether you're doing things that inadvertently hold you back

How do you succeed in life? Well, that's pretty ambitious of me to answer in one post, so let's dial it back: How do you succeed in your career?

I learned most of these lessons leading a global team of ambitious professionals. I realized it's much easier to see others' flaws than to see our own. An individual may struggle to see exactly what is holding them back. But rest assured, others can see it.

Some people feel unhappy with their careers because they are stuck with the notion that success means movement and change. How can you be successful if you haven't been promoted recently? Are you successful if you work for the same company for ten years? If your salary has not gone up every year?

The wisdom of your goals is yours to decide. But no matter your definition of success, I'm confident *you don't want to fail* at what you set out to do. Avoiding failure means identifying obstacles that may be standing in the way of you achieving your professional goals.

Are you doing things that are inadvertently hurting your career? If you find yourself answering "Yes" to any of the following questions, do not despair. I have thoughts on how to turn the tide.

1. Do you THINK mean things about your colleagues?

It is hard not to, right? People get on each other's nerves for all sorts of reasons. While you may believe you're good at keeping your thoughts to yourself, if you think mean or uncharitable thoughts about your colleagues, you can expect them to pick up on it.

They may not be able to say what exactly it is, but they will feel it. If you think mean thoughts, your interactions with colleagues will be negatively impacted.

2. Do you SAY mean things about your colleagues?

It can seem harmless to vent a little frustration. Especially since the person you are commiserating with has the same impression as you. We all know people who are unpleasant to work with: selfish, stubborn, incompetent even.

When you say negative things about others, even if your observations are accurate and richly deserved, you train the course of your thoughts to the negative. Worse, you are now the kind of person who says those thoughts to others. Your grandmother was right when she said, "If you don't have anything nice to say, don't say anything at all."

3. Do you focus ruthlessly on getting your own priorities accomplished?

You are busy, and you struggle to get your own work done. If you didn't focus on your priorities, then you would not be successful at all. Right?

Well, yes, actually, up to a point. Beyond just doing your job, however, you are presented with countless opportunities to make others' lives harder or easier. You can be selfish, focused only on yourself: "That's not my job."

What you may not notice is that others notice your selfishness. They often help each other because we all need help and we certainly appreciate receiving help.

If you never give help, don't be surprised if people are not quick to offer to help you.

4. Are you fixated on what your friends and colleagues earn?

Is your salary high? No idea. Is it higher than that of your friend? Easy answer. Such comparisons pave a predictable path to dissatisfaction.

If you spend your days comparing yourself to others, prepare to be unhappy most days. No matter how near the top you may have risen, you'll know someone else is always a bit closer.

5. Do you feel your pay isn't fair?

Fair is a magical word because everyone hearing it understands fairness differently. Thus, focusing on "fairness" is a recipe for sadness and frustration.

The world is not fair. Abilities and outcomes are unevenly distributed. Anyway, your conception of fairness is very different than other people's and highly influenced by what you want to achieve. Is it fair for you to be paid a higher salary? "Why certainly!" Is it fair for you to pay more taxes to help those less fortunate? "Don't be ridiculous."

If you feel you are not fairly paid, you will become resentful, impacting your attitude and work.

Ironically, one way to boost your salary is to stop obsessing about it. As you let go of the frustration and dissatisfaction, you will be happier. That will translate into your being a better colleague at work and doing better work. Which, of course, will over time translate into higher raises.

6. Do you think people less competent than you have been promoted ahead of you?

I've sat in on many promotion discussions. Trust me when I say your sense of others' abilities, accomplishments, and talents is incomplete. People get promoted for many reasons, some of which you may have no inkling of.

I've also offered a sympathetic ear to many employees who felt that others were unfairly promoted ahead of them. Whatever the reasons given, the unhappy employee is fixated on the idea that a less-deserving person has advanced ahead of them. (Maybe they have. It is useful to remember that sometimes life is not fair.)

But perhaps the promoted person deserved it, and you are unaware of all the circumstances. Your bitterness is evident to your colleagues and your boss. This makes them question your suitability for promotion yourself.

7. Do you feel that helping others is a distraction from your own work?

This is similar to point 3 but with this difference: The person focused on their own priorities is just busy, and perhaps oblivious to the harm being self-centered has on their relationship with colleagues. Such a person can come to realize that they need their colleagues to succeed.

If, however, you think helping others is a distraction, then you are likely to be not just self-centered but selfish in your interactions with them. You treat the workplace as a zero-sum game, where others' success comes at the expense of your own.

This is not a recipe for being considered a "team player." Nor an attitude that will win you your colleagues' admiration.

Change the frame by enlarging the scope of your ambitions. You are not working for narrow personal goals but for the good of the company. If helping the other person provides a greater benefit than focusing on your own task at that moment, your choice is easy.

8. Have you switched companies regularly (every three years or less)?

This can come from the sometimes misguided belief that success in your career requires motion. There is some truth to this. I have seen people job-hop their way to outrageous title inflation, far quicker than persons who stay in one place and do not agitate for change.

The trick is to find the balance between staying in one place long enough to learn the job and have an impact and switching rapidly to meet your own timetable of advancement. I know it is arbitrary, but for me switching companies every three years is too frequent.

As a hiring manager, if I see three or more such hops, I assume one of two things: this person has an unrealistic sense of how quickly their career should progress, and/or this person is a poor performer and has had to leave once each new employer figures it out. Either way, you are not an attractive hire for me.

9. Are you jealous of others' success?

Objectively seen, another person's success typically has very little or nothing to do with your own. Someone the same age as you is: a CEO, married to a fashion model, invested in a startup and became wealthy, or _____ fill in your own personal blank. Does that say anything at all about you?

No, it does not. And yet, it feels like it does. In our beating hearts, in the dark of night, others' success makes us feel less successful by comparison.

We forget the countless others we have ourselves surpassed. In these moments, we neglect to consider all we have to be thankful for. Envy will eat us up from the inside and leave only a bitter-tasting shell behind.

10. Do you focus on the negative in a situation more often than the opportunities?

One of my mottoes in life is "Be happy with what you have, not sad for what you don't have." I am not recommending that you be delusional or ignore bad things in your life.

No matter the situation, you are faced with a choice. Do you try to identify something positive about it? Or do you dwell on everything that is not perfect? You may not be able to easily identify something good in a situation. But I can promise you this: if you live in the land of perceived imperfection, you will be unhappy.

A person who can find something positive in dark times is wonderful to be around. A person who does this and shares their positive perspective is exactly who you want on your team. Because a crisis is always just around the corner.

I want people who are happy and positively inclined on my team and in my life. Because they will make a bad situation better, in ways that the doomsayer never could.

Some final advice

I don't know anyone without flaws. Many of my colleagues who would have answered Yes to some of the above nonetheless experienced fantastic results.

That's because to find career success your task is not to be perfect. Your task is to be self-aware and deliberate in how you approach situations.

Armed with this list, perhaps you will pick one idea and apply continuous improvement principles to tip the odds of success in your favor. Slowly but surely, you can turn the tide to your advantage.

Be well.

Chapter Seventeen

What I Learned from Judging and Being Judged

The best learnings I made over my career came from people who trusted me enough to tell me when I screwed something up

B eing judged can be painful, depending on how you are performing and how your reviewer delivers feedback. I've learned a lot about making good use of constructive criticism, which I'll share with you here.

I also realized in my years judging the finalists for the Association of Corporate Counsel's Top 10 30-Somethings that serving as a judge of others is not easy, especially if you're interested in being fair, constructive, and honest.

When I say I've learned something about judging, I also mean the process of giving and receiving feedback more generally and not just formal judging.

I hope you find something relevant and useful for your own development.

Which feedback is most valuable to you

There are two kinds of feedback you should delight in receiving:

- Feedback that comes from people whose opinions you respect and trust, and

- Feedback that is true regardless of the source.

The corollary to these rules is that you can apply a healthy skepticism to all other feedback you receive over your career.

Just because someone is sitting in a position to judge you does not necessarily (1) make them better than you, (2) give them meaningful insights into your performance, or (3) mean they know how to give constructive feedback.

A person whom you trust and respect, however, does you a great service when they give you feedback.

Even when, perhaps especially when, they tell you things that are painful, and where you have fallen short in your performance.

- This person is not trying to hurt you. Exactly the opposite. They care about you and are trying to help you get better.

- Treat this feedback like the gift it is and thank them for it.

- Then think about it and turn it to your advantage.

The best learnings I made over my career came from people who trusted me enough to tell me when I screwed something up.

What about people you don't trust, whom you may suspect are trying to cause you pain or trouble?

Here too, you can take advantage of the situation.

You do so by knowing your own strengths and weaknesses and having a healthy dose of self-awareness and self-confidence. Ask yourself the following question: "Is what this person is saying true?"

Even if their aim is to hurt you, by drawing attention to a real weakness, they have done you a service.

And if you are confident what the person is saying is not true, you are well-positioned to dismiss the person and their criticism, preserving your peace of mind.

Why perceived effort is a dangerous benchmark

I have observed that we are each usually the heroes of our own stories. We know our intentions are good, and we believe in the correctness of what we're doing.

This is only sensible and helps us get through hard times. But our natural human tendency can blind us to some objective truths.

- Sometimes we don't really put in enough effort to be successful in a project. We might be busy with other things, or not particularly motivated about this topic at this time.

- Or maybe we let emotions get the better of us. There are many reasons for not performing our best every now and then.

The thing is, work feels like work to us whether it is productive and on-task or whether we're wasting our time.

Work also feels like work to us without regard to the result. That is, the hours you spend negotiating a contract that fails to come to fruition are still hours of your life you will never get back.

Perhaps most relevant, the amount of effort we feel like we're investing is subjective.

- What seems like a huge effort to us may be trivial to a colleague.

- Maybe you are not as experienced or skilled, such that the same task that they think nothing of completing seems herculean to you.

Just because you think you're working hard does not mean you are performing well objectively.

Be well.

Chapter Eighteen

What Makes You Really Stand Out

First, a hard truth: Just being in difficult times doesn't make you special

How should we think about the extraordinary circumstances we find ourselves in, what are our personal convictions worth, and what is it that makes us unique?

This continues our exploration of lessons to be learned from judging and being judged (see the prior chapter), including giving and receiving feedback more generally.

What extraordinary circumstances say about us

First, a hard truth: Just being in difficult times doesn't make you special.

Although you may have been the person leading your company's COVID-19 response, or EU General Data Protection Regulation (GDPR) implementation, guess what? Every company was facing the same extraordinary times.

But let's say your extraordinary circumstance is less common: A hostile takeover attempt or major acquisition, bet-the-company litigation, or a serious regulatory inquiry.

This type of event never happens to many companies, or perhaps once in a few decades. So, it is genuinely extraordinary for you and your company. But it is not extraordinary for all in-house counsel. Right now, lots of companies are facing each of these issues.

I am sure your work was outstanding under the circumstances. But don't expect me to grade you higher *just because you responded to a crisis.* Remember, your comparison group is everyone else who was responding to the same or similar crises, not all the people on the sidelines.

Now the good news. A crisis presents excellent opportunities for you to stand out, even among all the people dealing with similar crises.

- How many contingencies did you manage to adequately plan for?

- How quickly did you identify the issue?

- How well did you convince skeptical colleagues that the company needed to act?

- And, ultimately, how well did you navigate your company through the shoals and to safer waters?

In sum, extraordinary circumstances of themselves say little about you. Even what may be unique in your company's history is mundane across the in-house landscape.

What makes you shine is how you respond to your circumstances.

What caring deeply about an issue is worth

The best in-house counsel are great people. They have broad interests and passionate convictions. They want to do more than help their companies succeed; they want to help their companies make the world a better place.

And there are rich opportunities in today's environment for us to do so. There are pressing climate change concerns, an extensive list of UN Sustainable Development Goals, and newfound commitments to diversity and inclusion.

I am delighted that you care deeply about these issues. I am tickled pink that you are on your company's diversity, equity, and inclusion (DEI) committee.

But, unless you turn your caring into concrete action, however, it's not worth much to me.

Remember our discussion earlier about the difference between effort and impact? The environmental, social, and governance (ESG) space is filled with a great deal of noise and little concrete results.

Don't misunderstand me. Passion is the engine that drives progress. Without your conviction and that of others like you, we are lost.

But your passion is the cover charge for this particular event. It gets you in the door.

- The people who stand out are the ones who focus their passion and demonstrate persistence in the face of resistance.

- It's hard enough to drive results without prioritizing attention and effort.

- So, pick a topic and stay with it until you see positive results. Then stick with it some more.

What makes us unique

Now that I've poured cold water on what you living through hard times and your passion tells us about your performance, let me spend a moment talking about the mundane challenges all in-house counsel face.

We spend most of our time developing efficient contracting systems, implementing compliance programs, and training our non-lawyer colleagues. Of course, we know that the best lawyers partner with the business in achieving business goals in a sustainable way.

If these challenges and opportunities are near-universal, what makes us stand out? One good place to look is our impact on those around us.

- Do you consistently help others thrive?

- Are people happier after spending time with you?

- Will people say about you, "She helps make the world a better place"?

When you find yourself answering yes to these questions, you are probably making your best contribution. An inspiring leader has an impact far greater than any amount of individual work can hope to accomplish.

I've now shared with you the key lessons I learned from judging and being judged, and in giving and receiving feedback.

I know some of the messages can seem a bit hard. But I hope by now you trust me enough to consider the truth of the matter in each case.

I also hope you trust yourselves enough to take only those lessons that apply to you and not take me so seriously on the lessons that don't. After all, you aren't like anyone else and that's one more thing that makes you special.

Be well.

Chapter Nineteen

Who's Running the Show of Your Life?

Are good things that happen the result of your agency, while bad things are caused by something other people did?

I've noticed something interesting about some successful people. They are the first ones to promote the idea that people are in charge of their own destiny. That with hard work and sacrifice you too can be successful.

They may espouse a corollary belief, which is that people who do not achieve all they want are simply lazy or lack intelligence or drive. But take such a person and ask them to explain a prominent failure they were associated with.

- "That wasn't my fault," you will hear.

- They trot out a thousand explanations and excuses, all of which point anywhere but them.

The takeaway is clear: Good things that happen are the result of their agency. Bad things are caused by something other people did.

Which group are you in?

I don't mean to pick on successful people. I've observed many unsuccessful people say the same thing. It's just they have fewer accomplishments to feel smug about, so you don't notice their inconsistency as much.

Let us refer to the inconsistent situational thinkers, whether successful or not, as the **Fair Weather Flock**.

Some smaller number of people are at least consistent in their thinking, although they fundamentally diverge into two groups in their approaches to life. Let's call the first group the **Things Just Happen** adherents and the other group **I Make Things Happen**.

Do you count yourself among either group? Here's how to tell.

You can distinguish members of the **Things Just Happen** group from the Fair Weather Flock in this way: They never add the words "to me" to their inner thoughts.

You will never hear them say "This bad thing happened to me," or "This good thing happened to me." Things just happen, it's not personal, and members of this group deal with it.

You might also think of this group as realists or fatalists. They don't control the cards that life deals them, but they find a way to make the best of the hand they've got.

What's refreshing about their approach to life is you don't usually hear them complaining. Life is what it is, sometimes great, often unfair, but they get on with managing their affairs.

Working with different styles

A member of the **Things Just Happen** tribe is great to have on your team because they are rarely fooled by wishful thinking. They see the world as it is, and they respond accordingly.

But this comes with some potential downsides. When you see the world as it is you can become cynical because we're surrounded by unfairness. The result can be a lack of initiative and less motivation to take on big challenges.

If the world is screwed up and out of our control, why should you go the extra mile?

Consider now the happy members of the **I Make Things Happen** group. You can also think of them as optimists, dreamers, and even naïve. They are certainly more likely to see the world through tinted glasses. On the positive side, they assume they control their destiny. They believe that with persistence and determination, they can make their own success.

This can-do attitude also makes them great team members. They are prone to putting in extra effort and consequently, they achieve great things more often than not.

When the Fair Weather Flock observes the successes of the I Make Things Happen group, they grumble, "They were just lucky," noting neither how this is inconsistent with how the Fair Weather Flock assesses their own performance nor how the I Make Things Happen group's luck always seems to go in only one direction.

But the I Make Things Happen members also suffer. Even the most determined people do not succeed at everything. And when failure strikes, members of this group feel it personally. They believe there must have been something more they could have done to avert the problem.

Pros and cons of the different groups

When I started this article, I thought I would declare a clear winner. For example, the I Make Things Happen group is more likely to be successful so the lesson would be that you should strive to take ownership of your life.

But I see that membership in each comes with pros and cons:

- **Fair Weather Flock**: Inconsistent and delusional, but happier by virtue of taking credit for good things while not taking the bad personally.

- **Things Just Happen**: The most accurate perception of the world, so avoids many wishful thinking mistakes but can miss out on opportunities that require hard work.

- **I Make Things Happen**: Consistent and delusional, most likely to be successful by virtue of taking more chances, but their sense of responsibility means balance and life satisfaction are harder to find.

Membership in these groups is not fixed or exclusive. Although I think most people tend towards one inclination most of the time, I have seen people purposefully change the course of their lives and careers by choosing another group.

Change requires two steps: Audit your past thinking to see whether you consistently assess the causes of both positive and negative events in your life; and make a conscious choice to assign agency for everything that happens in your life.

Your choices are these: I'm running the show (as long as times are good), no one's running the show, and it's always me running the show.

Choose wisely.

Be well.

Chapter Twenty

Sit Down and Stay Awhile*

Getting better at your job often leads to sustainable career success. I can't say the same about people who pursue a new job whenever it's dangled in front of them

I f you want to advance in your career, there's never been a better time to make a leap. Higher pay, flexible hours, and work from anywhere are all yours for the asking. There's certainly less justification to put up with a bad boss, an underperforming company, or missing development opportunities.

And yet, if you're not suffering from a significant disadvantage where you are, I'm going to advise you to think about staying put for a while longer.

Whether you stay or go really depends on whether you want merely career progress or to get better at your job. They are not necessarily the same. I find getting better at your job often leads to sustainable career success. I can't say the same about people who pursue a new job whenever it's dangled in front of them.

Often, the bigger job at the new company actually sets you back, at least in terms of your effectiveness. Why is that, you ask?

Success requires much more than specific expertise

For lawyers, what makes you effective in your job is a lot more than your legal skills. Knowing the law and how to apply it is of course important, but many good lawyers can do that.

What makes for a great in-house counsel is efficiently helping your company achieve its strategic objectives. Your core contribution to this goal is helping your company identify and navigate relevant risks. Here's how you do that.

Know the business

You first need to understand well what your company wants to accomplish from a business perspective. This is not trivial for lawyers, because you need to get out of your lawyer mindset and think more like you've got a master's in business administration (MBA).

Your business colleagues will have a long list of items, some vital to the company's success and others less so. You can't make useful risk assessments unless you understand the importance of the various business projects to the business. You will spend more time and be more creative in designing a risk-based approach when the project is critical. And you will be less tolerant of excess risk when a project is merely "nice to have."

Stay out of trouble

Similarly, how do you know what sorts of things are likely to get your company in trouble?

- Well, regulators themselves give you hints by the pace and scope of their rulemaking, as well as when they make public comments.

- Politicians do the same, usually by ratcheting up pressure on regulators.

- And if you're lucky, authorities will investigate and penalize other industry participants before you.

All this gives you warnings about what's hot and where you need to focus.

Work well with others

Next, because you are just one person, the amount you can do directly is limited. Thus, every manager is ultimately measured by how well they work with and through others.

For legal counsel, you more than most need to get your colleagues to do what you want them to. That's doubly hard because what you want often goes against their incentives and inclinations.

- You want salespeople to pay attention to contract terms even though that makes getting new business harder and takes longer.

- All employees need to be compliant and follow the law, even though this adds administrative burdens to their daily work.

Thus, you need to be great at building relationships. When your senior management team not only understands but is fully bought into your legal priorities, they will help you implement them. They will do this because they see the value to the company in what you're trying to accomplish, not just the costs.

You don't need everyone on your side, but you certainly can't do it alone.

There's likely much to learn and do where you are

I got better at my job every year for 20 years. You never stop finding ways to understand better your company and its business.

Every year makes you sharper in assessing which risks are the ones you need to focus on. And with every relationship you build and deepen, you expand your effective reach. Last but not least, you may feel immensely satisfied seeing the results of your hard work pay off over years.

Now consider the frequent job hopper. Even if they stay within their known industry, and many do not, they are but novices when it comes to many important things relating to their new company:

- The history that led to the current strategy

- Relationships among management and the board

- Whose opinion is respected and which others have the potential to cause trouble for you?

It's a long list of things you need to learn when you switch companies before you have any hope of being as effective as you were at your old company. The shiny new title (and let's not forget, higher pay) frequently blinds us to how much harder and riskier our jobs are in the early years. That is, there are costs and tradeoffs when taking that new job.

I know some remarkable people who have gone from strength to strength, who seem to be effective from the first day in a new job. These people are pretty rare in my experience. You may be one of them.

For all the rest of us, we owe it to ourselves to think about how effective we've become in our current jobs and why. Our self-reflection may inspire us to stay around a little longer.

Far from being a cop-out, deciding to stay at a company where you perform well demonstrates good judgment *and* courage.

Be well.

* This is a conversation I would have liked to have with every colleague I worked with over the years who was tempted to leave the company. Better late than never.

Chapter Twenty-One

The Worst Career Advice I've Seen in Ages

The happiest people I know are the ones who learn that success is not measured in money

I've noted before that bad advice is plentiful. Still, I was stunned to read in an otherwise respectable publication what I think is quite possibly the worst career advice ever.

The Wall Street Journal published an article about job switcherswith the subheading *"Even if you're happy at your job, getting a new job for more pay is a good strategy as inflation eats into paychecks."*

I've come across similar advice elsewhere: Always go after the bigger paycheck; your future raises build off your base salary, so target the highest-paying job; titles matter more than substance, so grab the CEO title if you want to earn the big bucks.

To be clear, this advice is spot-on if you want to make more money. But it is fantastically wrong-headed if you want to be happy in life.

The Journal article discusses data from the Federal Reserve Bank of Atlanta indicating that job switchers saw raises of 6.4%, while job stayers saw increases of only 4.7%.

Never mind that such a gap is not unusual. There is almost always a spread between job switchers and stayers, and job switchers typically increase their salary as part of a switch.

I have three objections to the idea of switching jobs just to make more money.

1. We are selfish employees if we think of our jobs only insofar as they meet our needs

2. We become more effective at our jobs with specific experience in our jobs

3. It is dangerously misleading to reinforce the idea that making more money (beyond a fairly low level) will improve your life satisfaction

1. Your job is about more than just you

The directors of a company serve at the pleasure of shareholders, and the officers serve at the pleasure of the board of directors. Although D&Os are typically handsomely paid for their service, they have clear fiduciary duties to the constituents whose interests they serve.

I don't expect every employee to have the same feelings of fiduciary duty. It is reasonable to expect, however, employees to identify with and wish to see their companies succeed.

If you find yourself believing that your company owes you something and you owe nothing in return, you are a bad employee.

2. You need time to get good at your job

There are more than enough people with the raw talent to do most jobs. What makes a person stand out as a top performer? It is when they know enough about their company, colleagues, and culture to effectively drive strategic initiatives.

Good ideas are plentiful. The ability to implement good ideas is rare indeed. This requires a mix of realism, humility, and doggedness that most people never find. The people who do develop this mix typically do so only after some years on the job.

- They learn about their company's history, including its past successes and failures.

- They identify the respected voices, those people who can help speed a project along or, conversely, stop one in its tracks.

- They learn how an initiative fits with the company's overall strategy, finding opportune times to push when they know they'll find a tailwind.

People who switch jobs every few years learn none of this. They forever run up against walls they don't even understand.

Ironically, this makes them more likely to switch jobs again, before frustration and burnout (and their own lack of results) derail them.

3. Making money is a means, not an end

Some of the most ambitious people I know would seem to have the least to complain about. Generous six-figure salaries, comfortable work environments, and enviable lifestyles.

And despite their objective advantages, they are tempted by a higher salary, an ostensible promotion, and a new company. It's as if they feel compelled to pursue the objective markers for success.

When I ask, "Will making more money change your life in meaningful ways?" or "What is it that makes you successful in your current job, and will you have the same advantages in your new one?" they don't have ready answers.

The happiest people I know are the ones who learn that success is not measured in money:

- Can you say you like, trust, and respect the people you work with?

- Is your work interesting, challenging, and valuable?

- And do you share values with a solid company that has a strategy for continued success?

Then you have all you need to be happy and successful in your career. And if you find yourself in that position, why would you give up a great job for a little more money or even a lot more money?

If you do, you risk getting not only what you want but what you deserve.

Be well.

Chapter Twenty-Two

You Can't Buy Accountability

And that's why it's so sought after in companies

I 've had a bias in favor of in-house counsel for years. These are lawyers who work as employees of a single company. It seemed to me that in-house counsel have many advantages over outside counsel, meaning lawyers who work in a law firm for many clients.

I admit that when I worked in private practice at a law firm, I had the exact opposite view. Outside counsel are in the business of delivering legal advice. As such, I thought, they've got greater focus, specialization, and expertise. Also, why would clients pay hundreds of dollars an hour for them to answer questions if not for the brilliance?

I spent only five years in private practice, but that was long enough to realize our clients carried many motives. Most had properly difficult issues that needed our thorough and expensive attention.

Many clients, however, seemed to use our services for other reasons: As overflow capacity, to handle bothersome tasks, or to provide credibility in potentially risky cases.

When I took up the General Counsel role in my company, I soon found all three reasons to be objectionable. Let's consider them in turn.

Overflow capacity: Legal needs aren't so unpredictable

Every legal team deals with a reasonably predictable workload, alongside the terrifying unpredictable matters that lurk behind random phone calls and emails.

Combining both work types can make it seem like our total workload itself is unpredictable. But this is not so for at least two reasons.

1. Predictable work is just that: predictable. No matter what other distractions arise, the regular needs of the business must be met. Depending on your business, this work likely constitutes 60–80 percent of the workload.

2. Unpredictable work is unpredictable only in the specific details and not in *whether* unpredictable things will occur.

Over time I came to realize that, while I couldn't say exactly when, for example, an employee dispute would crop up, or what form it would take, we would have a certain number of them.

Or that, although significant customer or supplier disputes were rare, they did occur. And eventually, almost all the matters that I once would have called a surprise were anything but.

This means that a legal team's workload is mostly foreseeable, most of the time. Seeking outside help for work that is reasonably foreseeable, and paying handsomely for the flexibility, seemed to me like an expensive luxury. And because I sought to deliver value to my company, I soon viewed such capacity buying as an avoidable luxury.

Whenever our outside counsel spending exceeded a certain threshold, I'd make the case for hiring an in-house resource to do the work ourselves. I originally made the business case on financial terms, because the payoff was immediate.

Only later did I realize my business colleagues valued in-house lawyers fundamentally differently. More on this in a moment.

Bothersome tasks: Doing unglamorous work is part of the job

Yes, I get it. We all want to do exciting, innovative, and important work. It takes experience and maturity to understand a lot of important work is neither exciting nor innovative. It's up to team leaders to make employees see the value in doing unglamorous but important work.

Although some employees are more willing to go along than others, don't be a lazy manager and take advantage of them. The right way to dole out important work is the same way to divvy up exciting work: A roughly equal share that gives everyone similar opportunities to contribute and develop.

And as the team leader, that means you should do a fair share of unglamorous work too. I know that with seniority comes some perks, which includes being able to assign less desirable work to team members. Do this too often and you become the boss you once hated.

It is also being a lazy manager if you foist off unglamorous work to outside counsel. Not only is this more expensive, they see it as unglamorous too and push it down to the least experienced associate. What makes you think that's an appropriate way to get important work done well?

And before you tell me that much unglamorous work is also unimportant, I would say that your legal strategy surely has identified and eliminated unimportant work in favor of proper priorities.

Buying credibility: Going outside risks selling your own credibility short

When you have significant matters before you, you may be tempted to call on outside counsel for expertise, moral support, and authority. Often this is the right call, especially when you are in an unfamiliar legal domain. Be careful, though, and don't call on outside help to make decisions for you.

You have one thing even the most expert outside counsel lacks, and the business knows it: Accountability.

Outside counsel are your hired guns. But the company they're defending is your home, where you spend most of your time, and where your friends also work. When outside counsel's work is done, they ride off, having been paid either way. You live with the consequences.

The best outside counsel appreciate this dynamic and support their in-house colleagues. They collaborate closely with you behind the scenes so that when you make recommendations to management about what to do next, they are *your* recommendations.

This is not an ego question so much as a judgment question. Nothing can take the place of your deep knowledge of your company's business and risk appetite.

Thus, the most important thing you bring to the table as in-house counsel is ownership. When you own your decisions, and your colleagues know it, that brings you credibility money can't buy.

Be well.

Chapter Twenty-Three

Sweet CEO Lies: "Employees Are Our Most Valuable Asset"

I'll tell you what CEOs genuinely believe but will never say out loud

F or everyone worried about DOGE firing large swathes of government employees, there was an earlier precedent when he took over Twitter. Almost everyone agreed Musk was making a huge mistake when swung his giant scythe at the employee ranks of Twitter. Reports suggest he fired as many as 80% of Twitter's employees.

How could this not have an immediate detrimental effect on shareholder value? Wasn't he just killing the company quickly rather than slowly like everyone assumed he would?

The people who *didn't* think Musk was risking much (then or now) included those who've managed large teams of employees in big U.S. corporations. We know something about the truth of that much-hyped ending to many CEO's annual shareholder letters:

> *I want to thank our hardworking employees. Employees are our most valuable asset.*

Employees are far from equal

What we know (and what every CEO knows but will never say) is the following:

- About 10% of employees have a real impact

- A bit more than half are better to have than not

- The rest are either not pulling their weight or are downright harmful

You can also think of it this way: 10% of employees generate 80% of the value, and another 5% generate 80% of the problems.

You can probably remember being around employees who massively drive progress. Because you're reading this, you're more likely to be one of those employees. Congratulations!

I spent a career as a corporate lawyer dealing with the 5% who generated most of the problems. They're real and preventing them from harming your company is seriously time-consuming.

The problem every company faces is how to reliably find out which employees are which. Performance evaluations are all but useless, given the exaggeration and self-serving lying that occurs by everyone. Waiting for trouble to arise is also risky.

Musk was looking for a way to quickly sort employees

Musk's method was quick and brutal, so necessarily was imperfect. But it seems clear he was trying to identify who were the top and bottom employees by forcing them to self-select.

No slacker or outright troublemaker was going to sign up for 80-hour weeks of in-office pressure and unrelenting work. Was there a risk Musk would lose some of his best performers as well? Of course. But he almost certainly cut out a cancer that would have slowly killed Twitter just as his detractors hoped.

What about the great majority of employees in the middle, who are neither superstars nor super-shitty? Here we come to the lie in every CEO's letter to shareholders about employees being the company's most valuable asset.

- The truth is, that companies are far stronger when they can identify and remove the 5% harmful subversives and the 15–25% disengaged and lazy.

- Moreover, because every large organization is a morass of bureaucracy and inefficiency, half of the average employees are functionally unnecessary or performing tasks that don't materially help the company.

One reason so many people hate Elon Musk is that he is willing to do things that uncomfortably disrupt the status quo. If his company can survive just fine with 20% of its employees, what does that suggest about the staffing of other large companies? Or the U.S. government?

What are a company's most valuable assets?

There's a pretty clear accounting answer to this question. Your feelings for Mr. Musk aside, a company's financial statements reveal the value of their various assets.

Employees are not even close to the most valuable asset at most companies. The list looks more like this:

1. The company brand

2. Intellectual property around the products and services

3. New products and services

4. Customer relationships

5. Legacy products and services

6. Supplier relationships

… Employees are usually in the top ten, though.

If you want your company to think you're really valuable, it helps to be honest about where you fall on the curve.

Be well

Chapter Twenty-Four

How To Manipulate CEOs

This is something writers are especially well-positioned to do

I was several years into my executive role as head of legal for a large public company when I realized my fellow managers were idiots, none more so than the CEO.

I don't mean they sucked at their jobs or lacked education, experience, or skills. Far from it. These were capable, well-trained, and effective individuals. It's just that they suffered from a common flaw that afflicted their decision-making. Worse yet, they were completely unaware of it.

Did this mean individuals could take shameless advantage of the blind spot whenever they needed to influence a manager's thinking? I'll leave the answer to your imagination.

The method is simplicity itself. I share it with you today not so you can manipulate others but to help ensure others don't make a fool of you.

Stories carry disproportionate weight in persuasion

The blind spot is this: We all like to think we are rational, logical decision-makers but we are not. We make decisions based on emotions and effortlessly rationalize our decisions. Thus, an easy way to influence someone's decision is to hijack their emotions.

Nothing arouses emotions better than a story. You'd think this has little traction in the business context because who has time for long-winded stories?

That's where anecdotes come in. All you need is a single customer remark and you've got powerful juju in your hands.

Let's say you want to cause trouble for a colleague who is showing dangerous competence and ambition. They've recently rolled out a new customer-facing app. Here's what you do:

- Casually remark to your colleague's boss that you heard customers were complaining about glitches in the new app.

- Pro tip: Enlist an ally to make a similar offhand comment a few days later.

- Then sit back and watch the anecdote turn into reality.

The reason this works is because emotions are in play. The boss is secretly worried that their smooth ascent will be interrupted and they'll be found out as a fraud. Nothing reveals their lack of substance so much as disgruntled customers. At the merest whiff of discontent, they'll scatter like chickens before a hungry fox.

The rival who rolled out the app is sorely disadvantaged. That's because there's always somebody who dislikes change. They'll be complaining no matter how great the new app is. Furthermore, to claim that no customer had problems is not believable and will undermine the rival's credibility.

Even worse for them, if they try to present data to counter the point, they'll come across as defensive. You cannot fight anecdotes with logic or data.

How to recognize when someone's using the method on you

Whenever someone refers to general feedback from customers in vague terms, chances are excellent they're trying to trick you with anecdotes. Either that or they've themselves been fooled by someone who applied the method to them.

Here's an example from the writers' platform, Medium. In one of their Writer Newsletters, the VP of Content said this:

> *The goal of the Medium Partner Program is to deliver value to readers and writers, and **we often hear from our members** that these kinds of stories ["meta" stories about Medium itself] aren't the*

*ones they want to read, much less pay for. You're free to write meta
stories, we just don't want Partner Program funds going to them.
Payments seem to incentivize extra navel gazing and unwanted
get-rich-quick culture.* [emphasis added]

Did you catch the misdirection? "We often hear from readers..." Oh really? I
would bet you a considerable sum that this is pure anecdote driving emotions
used to support a pre-determined outcome.

There are several indications to support this:

- How exactly does Medium solicit feedback from writers or readers?
  Moreover, those who submit unsolicited feedback have found
  themselves handily rebuffed.

- How many writers craft "meta" stories precisely because they have
  historically been their most popular stories? More engagement, more
  comments, and active interest from readers and writers alike.

- Of all the types of stories people supposedly don't want to read, why is
  it that management throttles "meta" stories? There's smut and poetry
  and politics and any number of topics that people don't like. For all
  these, we're told to click "less like this" and the problem is solved. But,
  uniquely, readers and writers alike can't figure out how to see fewer
  "meta" stories.

- Medium reveals their hidden emotions with the last sentence — note the
  phrase "extra navel gazing and unwanted get-rich-quick culture." This is
  management saying what IT wants, not what writers and readers want.
  Half of the work on Medium consists of navel-gazing and the other half
  is get-rich-quick hacks.

Medium's animus to criticism from members is further reflected in its
Distribution Guidelines: "We also often see inaccurate speculation or advice and
are not able to respond in every case." Got it? Misinformation shall be censored
in the name of a "better internet." That this also hides information critical of
management is entirely coincidental.

Medium can do what it likes. What they cannot do is pretend they are simply
delivering what readers and writers wish.

Medium is doing what IT wants, namely reducing distribution (censoring) stories that raise questions about what management itself is doing. We see you.

Two methods to fight the tactic

You can fight back with anecdotes of your own. This will not win any arguments but will blunt the force of one-sided anecdotes.

If you have the time and money, you can gather data to refute a misleading anecdote. This is risky because you will be confronted with motivated reasoning. That is, people believe what they want to believe and handily fit evidence to their preconceptions.

You are thus wise if you first explore the hidden motivations of management and your colleagues. What do they secretly believe or wish to be true? If you can play to and reinforce existing beliefs (or fears or wishes, etc.) you will find receptive ears.

Best of all, you don't need to be bound by data or facts in playing to a person's unstated beliefs. They are primed to believe you. You can freely concoct anecdotes of your own and they will go unchallenged.

I've heard from many writers that they're annoyed with the tone-deaf changes being rolled out by management.

Be well.

Chapter Twenty-Five

Maybe Attaining Work-Life Balance Isn't the Best Goal for You

Instead, deliberately choose when to be unbalanced

At one point several years into my General Counsel role for an S&P 500 public company, I wrote three letters up on my whiteboard. They were to serve as my guideposts for the rest of my career.

The letters were these: F H W.

My boss came in one day and asked "What're those?"

I told him they stood for Family, Health, and Work. I said that they represented my priorities in life, in that order.

He pondered my whiteboard and my statement for a few moments and said, "Those are nice goals ... for your next job."

Message clear. What got you here is what will keep you here. If you want an easy life, go get an easy job.

Balance and performance are like Clark Kent and Superman

That is, you generally don't see them together.

Nothing in my path to getting a C-suite job by my 30s was remotely the result of balance.

- *Family*: haha! I was single until my last year of law school. When I started working, I kept a picture of my wife nearby to remember what she looked like.

- *Social life*: You must be joking. In my law firm days, the only times I wasn't working I was desperate for sleep.

- *Exercise*: Yeah, right. I suppose carting boxes of prospectuses from the printer counted for something.

Okay, so I worked a lot more than was healthy. But I credit my rise in no small part to letting my life get well and truly out of balance in pursuit of high performance.

What about after you reach your goal? Can you find balance then?

That was my initial thought. *"Oh, when I'm experienced and powerful enough, I'll be able to find balance."*

It wasn't to be. But this story is no tragedy.

My epiphany leading to those three letters appearing on my whiteboard was suddenly realizing that I was mid-30s, overweight, out of shape, and likely heading for an early heart attack.

I resolved to adopt healthy habits, starting with losing weight. I approached this mission with abandon, which is to say completely unbalanced, shedding 50 pounds (ca. 23 kg) in six weeks.

Now, how to maintain a healthy weight? It seemed clear that exercise plus diet was a winning combination, so I started running while eating largely the same meals every single day.

This is about the time when I wrote the three letters on the board. At that moment, my focus was pretty clearly on the H part of the trio. I was going to be healthy no matter the cost.

That's why I ignored my boss and stuck with my exercise habit. And although I was prepared to be fired for my conviction, in the end, my company got a fine deal.

True, I was now spending an hour a day exercising that I could have been working. But the impact of working out at lunchtime was incredibly positive to my performance.

So positive that we introduced physical fitness as a key component of our global management training program.

Did you ever achieve balance?

Not really. But I think I achieved something better.

That is, I came to understand that life is about flux and change. I embraced the uncertainty and learned to work with it.

Nothing around us is static, fixed, or in balance. Why should our lives be? Life is punctuated by intense peaks and drudgerous flat stretches.

- Sometimes we're healthy and sometimes we're not. We can control a lot, but not everything.

- We enjoy tender and beautiful times with friends and family that carry us through the times we are apart.

- Work tosses up challenges that demand every bit of our attention and effort. It is also repetitive and boring and maddening.

- Maybe your fitness goals will require intense periods of training, leading you to temporarily neglect other areas of life.

The one caution I'd recommend is to *be deliberate in choosing when to be unbalanced*. I always knew when I was devoting unusual time in pursuit of a priority and made sure it was temporary.

I'll train hard for six months, but then family and work need to get their fair share. I'll work weekends to see an intense project to the finish line, but then I'll take my vacation.

In sum: Why being unbalanced is okay

If you seek high performance in one domain (work), you'll likely seek it in others.

Letting yourself become unbalanced in your pursuit of ambitious goals increases the odds you will achieve them.

To me at least, the thrill of achieving outrageous goals was worth giving up the improbable dream of balance.

Be well.

Chapter Twenty-Six

This 3-Step Method Can Help You Build Resilience

Remember, you can turn adversity into strength!

L earned everything valuable about resilience while working, including my twenty years leading the legal team of a multinational public company.

Then I retired and discovered I wasn't finished learning about resilience.

If work gave me two key components for building resilience, philosophy was the third piece that helped create a unified whole.

Here's how I'll share it with you:

- I describe what I mean by resilience.

- I offer a handy lens for making sense of the world.

- I share a simple method for building resilience.

- Lastly, we'll explore the method's application in three core areas: (1) your person, (2) your planning, and (3) your thoughts.

Resilience Means ...

A resilient person is strong, capable, and tough.

When the unexpected occurs, a resilient person is able to deal with every eventuality.

When hit with a setback, a resilient person bounces back quickly, even stronger.

How do you think about resilience? Would you add anything to these descriptions?

A handy lens for viewing the world: What's in your control?

Understanding the answer to this simple question helps you focus your efforts when building resilience.

Distinguish between things fully in your control, outside your control, and partially in your control.

Fully in our control: what we think, say, and do. (*Us, our person*)

Outside our control: the world and its random happenings, third parties (what others think, say, and do), and bad luck, such as weather and delays. (*What happens to us*)

Partially in our control: how prepared are we for what happens, how we respond to what happens, and our good fortune. (*How we respond to what happens*)

> *It is an invincible greatness of mind not to be elevated or dejected with good or ill fortune. A wise man is content with his lot, whatever it be — without wishing for what he has not.* — Seneca

A Simple Method for Building Resilience: Increase Your Control and Leverage What You Do Control

The more you assume responsibility, the more resilient you will be. If you are not the master of yourself, who is?

- Who controls your own person?

- Who controls what you know and can do?

- Who controls what you feel?

As you consider these questions, remember that things that appear outside your control may not be.

The unexpected is troublesome, true, but you can manage what you plan for. And even when you control little of your external circumstances, you still have control.

> *Knowing others is to be clever. Knowing self is to be wise. Overcoming others requires force. Overcoming self requires strength. Realizing contentment is wealth.* — Lao Tzu, Tao Te Ching

Let's explore your levers.

1. Your person — Make yourself strong, capable, and tough

You can make yourself stronger in three domains: your person, your abilities, and your attitude.

Your person: Adopt long-term healthy habits.

- Schedule time for fitness in your calendar

- Eat healthy, take time for lunch

- Get up and walk around periodically, e.g. every 90 minutes

- Get enough sleep, with consistent bedtimes and waking times

Your abilities: Continuously improve your skills.

- Take advantage of continuous improvement opportunities

- University courses, in-person and online

- Professional reading, podcasts

- Zen koan: "to a sincere student, every day is a fortunate day"

Your attitude: Cultivate a positive mindset. Simple habits can shape your personality.*

- Practice gratitude

- Maintain a journal

- Meditate briefly

- Engage with your social network

- Exercise (supporting the first point above)

You are a combination of your habits and the people who you spend the most time with. Many distinctions between people who get happier as they get older and people who don't can be explained by what habits they have developed. — Naval Rivikant

2. Your planning — Be prepared for any eventuality

Regain control over the unexpected using three simple tools.

Ask "what if" questions. You cannot be surprised by things you have anticipated.

Prepare contingency plans. You respond more quickly and effectively by giving yourself a head start when a crisis hits.

Here are some examples to illustrate.

Question: What if it rains today? Contingency plan: I will bring my raincoat and an umbrella.

Question: What if my train is late? Contingency plan: I will build extra time into my schedule and leave earlier.

Question: What if my company gets sued? Contingency plan: I've interviewed lawyers in advance and I know who I would call for each type of case.

Question: What if we have a problem with one of the products we sold? Contingency plan: I have product liability insurance.

The third tool is to learn to **be happy for small crises**. When you've anticipated and planned, you welcome the chance to practice. Here are the rules of thumb regarding crises:

- Anything you haven't planned for has the potential to become a big crisis.

- Anything that doesn't kill you is a small crisis.

- Your test is never the crisis itself, but how prepared you are to respond.

Those whose care extends not far ahead will find their troubles near at hand. — Confucius

3. Your thoughts— Become stronger in the face of setbacks

You regain control over your thoughts in the face of setbacks by asking yourself three questions:

1. **Did I plan for this situation?** Whenever you encounter a situation you've planned for, you have already succeeded.

2. **Is it really so bad?** So what if ... I get wet, I'm a few minutes late, my flight is canceled, etc.

3. **What's the upside case?**

The first two exercises are relatively easy. Answering the third question advances you from average practitioner to expert.

Make a game of finding the silver lining in apparent misfortune. It gets easier the more you do it.

- The rain is calming and cleans pollen from the air.

- My train/plane being late means I have more time to finish that podcast.

- This massive lawsuit means my priorities suddenly became clear.

Over time, you'll be able to find the positive in every situation: didn't get that big promotion, lost your car keys, sprained your ankle.

> *I have always believed, and I still believe, that whatever good or bad fortune may come our way we can always give it meaning and transform it into something of value.* — Herman Hesse

Summary of the three-step resilience method

Start by understanding what's in your control and what's not. Seek then to increase your control where possible and leverage the control you do have.

Your three areas of emphasis are as follows: your person, your planning, and your thoughts.

1. Make yourself strong, capable, and tough by being physically fit, pursuing continuous improvement opportunities, and cultivating a positive mindset.

2. Be prepared for every eventuality by asking what could happen and putting in place simple contingency plans.

3. Use your control over your thoughts to turn adversity into an advantage by always spotting the silver lining.

The wonderful news is that building resilience is within our control. When all others are losing their heads, we can be both calm and strong.

Be well.

Chapter Twenty-Seven

Most Advice Fails One of These Two Tests

Plus, why people don't take advice

W e've never had more advice available to us. How come everyone isn't wealthy, healthy, and happy as a result?

How come we aren't all making $10,000 a week without working, or attracting 100,000 views a day on our blog, or whatever else it is that our hearts desire?

I'll answer these questions by describing why most advice fails. I then offer a method for you to assess whether the advice you're considering is right for you.

Here's one reason people don't take advice

Asa corporate lawyer, my business was giving advice. As a General Counsel for twenty years, I got used to people following my advice — whether they wanted to or not.

Now I'm just one voice among thousands, writing publicly about how to achieve better outcomes. People are entirely free to take my advice or ignore it. I'll admit, I sometimes long for my authoritarian days.

I focus my writing on things I know best, which is what I've seen work in the real world over decades. (I list my core strengths below if you're curious.) I'm trying to limit myself to only solid advice. So why don't people take it every time?

Machiavelli has part of the answer. In describing rulers and their advisers in The Prince, Machiavelli said this:

There are actually three kinds of mind: one grasps things unaided, the second sees what another has grasped, and the third grasps nothing and sees nothing.

What group are you in?

This simple concept explains why the world is divided into an elite one percent, a highly effective 10 percent, and everyone else.

Only a tiny percentage of people are novel thinkers with great ideas. The next group can distinguish between great ideas and everything else, i.e., they can tell good advice from bad advice.

The final group is neither original nor discerning in their thinking — they are forever prone to making mistakes because they don't recognize or follow good advice. It's just not in their nature.

Can people change the group they're in?

Particularly if you don't start out naturally gifted, can you become a person who is able to at least identify good advice?

I'm convinced the answer is yes. (Otherwise, many of us are wasting a lot of our time trying to spread good advice.) How does one learn to identify good advice?

Do we trust a pundit because of their position or experience? Are we convinced by a good anecdote or testimonial? Do we want hard data backing up the expert's claims?

In preparing my own advice, I read lots of other people's advice. I can tell you, there's a great deal of excellent advice out there. But there's as much or more poor advice. Your first task is thus to identify advice worth considering.

Good advice must pass these two tests

    1. It must work at all

    2. It must work for you in your situation

Most advice fails one or both of these tests.

Advice that does not work *at all* is unquestionably poor advice. So why is it so common? It comes about because people repeat things they see frequently without exploring the underlying rationale.

To give you a few examples:

- **Pursuing your passion** is a great way to work hard while going broke. Some people will be successful, but it will be because of many factors beyond their passion.

- If you **just keep doing something**, eventually you will be successful. This fallacy gives rise to the immense profits of lottery operators and casinos. Not to mention the broken dreams of many a poet, pundit, or weather prognosticator. It's easy to see that most people will fail at many activities no matter how long they persist.

Advice that does not work *for you* is also poor advice, at least as far as you're concerned. This advice arises because people mistake anecdotes for evidence. That is, a well-meaning person says "This worked for me! Do what I did, and you will see the results I did."

Uh, almost certainly not. You won't get the results Tim Ferriss did by reading his books or listening to his podcast because you don't think like Tim Ferriss. You won't get Tim Denning's income by subscribing to his newsletter or taking his courses, because you don't write like Tim Denning.

We're fooled by such persons because they communicate engagingly and show a genuine desire to help. How can I not want to listen to someone successful and entertaining who is offering to help me?

What's a person looking for self-improvement to do?

You must apply critical thinking to any advice you're considering

1. Ask first, **does it look like this advice ever works for anyone?** What evidence do I have for this? Is it just folk wisdom that has been repeated endlessly, or is there any objective data I can assess?

2. Then ask, **what are the conditions** under which people have

successfully implemented this advice? For example— Does running a successful winery require $10 million in starting capital?— What percentage of investors beat their benchmark performance in any given year? What percentage do so over ten years? Are factors other than luck necessary to explain the results?— Is every person who just "writes every day" successful in time? Or is it that the large majority of writers stop, and some gifted ones continue on to success?

3. If you can identify conditions for success, be honest in assessing **whether those conditions apply in your case**. If not, that advice won't work for you. If yes, keep thinking.

4. Next, explore other reasons **why people have failed** trying to implement this advice. What external factors influenced their outcomes? What individual-specific factors drove results? And so on.

5. If you meet the base conditions for success and the likely reasons for failure do not apply to you, you are not done. Now ask, **what else did this person do** that contributed to their success? Is there companion advice that you must also consider?

This is starting to sound like hard work, even to me. It also explains why people have a hard time identifying good advice and then successfully implementing it.

But now you're armed with one method to determine whether someone's advice is good for you.

Be well.

Chapter Twenty-Eight

How to Measure Your Impact on the World

An explanation of the Purpose-Influence-Power Model for determining your impact on the world

D o you have an idea how you impact the world? Would you like to know how you compare on a relative basis?

We're living in times when individuals can reach more fellow humans than ever before. This is because the world's population has never been larger and our tools to reach others have never been more powerful. As a result, people today can do great good but also great harm.

The Purpose-Influence-Power Model gives us a helpful tool to examine individuals' relative impact. Let me explain a few terms and then we can fill in some details and try our model out.

What does Purpose mean?

Purpose means both what you are trying to achieve and the likely outcome, at least directionally. Important: *you don't get credit for good intentions alone.*

If you are trying to feed your family but you do so by selling drugs or stealing, you're trending towards the left side of the chart — causing harm. We say this even though your stated intention may be to help others, i.e. your family.

Similarly, if you say you want to help others, but you do so by establishing a charity that pays you a salary that consumes most of your donated funds, you belong in the self-focused column.

Think of purpose as intention plus effect, or your aim and the result you achieve.

What does Influence mean?

Influence means the number of people you can reach by your actions. How much good (or harm) can you do directly?

If you are selling vegetables from your garden, your reach is those people who buy your produce.

If you are a petty criminal, your reach is the people you victimize plus the follow-on victims. I.e., stealing from a parent also affects what they can provide for their family.

If you are sharing ideas with the world, your reach is everyone who comes across your idea. A sign on your lawn has less reach than a letter to the editor of your local paper. Your letter has less reach than a viral video.

What does Power mean?

Power also measures the number of people your actions affect, with the difference that power reflects what you can do *indirectly*.

Because you're the CEO, you can fire thousands of employees with a simple decision. If you're the President, you can sign legislation into law. When you're a billionaire philanthropist, you can direct charitable spending that affects millions.

Power versus Influence — Some distinctions

A person with influence tends to have power because their ideas spread. While they cannot force anyone to change their behavior, their ideas cause people to change how they think. Thus, influence is a form of indirect power.

A person with power tends to have influence. If nothing else, they can force you to bend to their will. Their power can be purely structural, meaning it comes largely from their office or position because individuals do not trust their ideas.

Alternatively, a person's structural power can be supported by their also having influential ideas. A billionaire CEO with 100 million Twitter followers has both structural power and indirect power via their influence.

The fun part — Filling in the chart

Now we can identify categories of people in the different areas of the Purpose-Influence-Power chart.

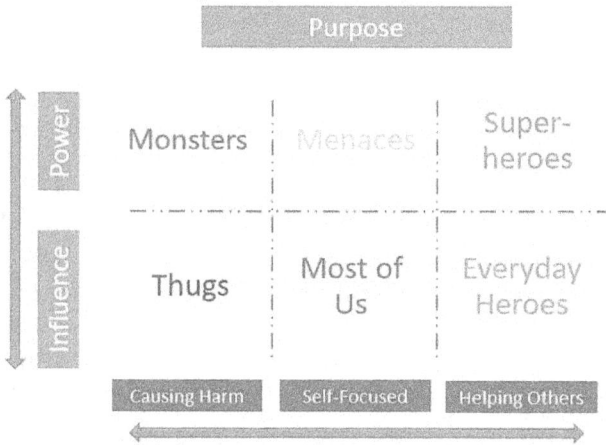

The Purpose-Influence-Power Model (c) James Bellerjeau

Most of Us

Most of us fall into the **Most of Us** category. We have limited influence or power and focus on our own problems. And that's totally OK. Because even without structural power or influential ideas, people can make the world worse.

Thugs

Those that cause intentional harm are Thugs. Thugs are plentiful, and include petty criminals, online scammers, and everyone else who decides to harm others or is indifferent to their suffering.

Everyday Heroes

At the other end are Everyday Heroes, people who make the world better by their actions. They include anyone who contributes to charity, volunteers their time, or takes any action to alleviate unnecessary suffering.

Menaces

As one's influence and power grow, the greater your opportunities for real impact. Menaces use their power and influence for selfish purposes. They miss an opportunity to do good but do not descend into active harm. Think of narcissistic politicians or oligarchs who selfishly spend their money on lavish indulgences.

Monsters

The other two extremes interest us, because their impact is great. Monsters have power and influence and cause harm to the world. As a reminder, intentions are not as important as impact, particularly when one has great power and influence.

- Mark Zuckerberg may have intended to connect the world, but his social media companies' have also sowed mistrust, misinformation, and division.

- Similarly, George Soros may have intended to advance social justice, but his progressive prosecutors have unleashed a crime wave on the unhappy victims he was most hoping to help.

Superheroes

This leaves us with the happy category of Superheroes, people who use their great power and influence with both the intention *and effect* of helping improve the world.

- Bill Gates and Warren Buffet are surely in this category thanks to their immense charitable contributions that have benevolent effects.

- It seems clear that Elon Musk belongs here as well. He generates resentment because of his power and influence, as do most in the top half of the chart. But Mr. Musk's intentions and his impact have been positive for humankind, at least so far.

Going forward we will fill in our chart with world leaders, politicians, celebrities, and more. Let me know someone you'd like to place on the Purpose-Influence-Power chart, and we can do it together.

Be well.

Chapter Twenty-Nine

Do You Overweight the Present at the Cost of the Future?

Most of us ignore the long-term effects of our individual daily decisions. But we can turn human nature to our advantage

A bird in the hand is worth two in the bush. Have you ever wondered why that is? The proverb reveals facets of human nature that lead most of us astray, but which can also be our salvation.

This proverb contains two truths:

- We value things we can have now more than things we will receive in the future

- We place even less weight on future outcomes if there is uncertainty about the future

The future is distant ... and murky

We know eating that donut is bad for us. But it sure tastes good! And we tell ourselves we took the stairs this morning. Plus, it was a stressful day and we deserve it, don't we?

This shows the problem with our daily habits: The connection between the donut today and our weight tomorrow, let alone a few months from now is virtually invisible. The same is true for a workout and our long-term fitness.

Put differently, the future value of a single decision today is highly uncertain. This helps explain why we fail the marshmallow test, i.e., we do not defer immediate gratification for a later gain.

At the same time, the *cumulative* effect of daily decisions we make over months and years is all too plain. If we spend more than we earn, we will rack up debt. If we do not exercise, we'll be unfit. We all know this, and yet we routinely manage to avoid thinking about it.

Two levers make the future feel more tangible

To make the future reward look more attractive relative to the present temptation, we can do the following:

1. Increase the perceived value of the future reward

2. Decrease uncertainty about the likelihood we will receive the reward

We can make a future reward more valuable by making it more personal and tangible. We don't intuitively feel we have much in common with our future selves. Maybe this is because we struggle to imagine that we will be old.

One way to overcome this failure of imagination is to age a photo of your current face. Several apps will do this. When you see a picture of your future aged face, you can much more easily imagine you will one day be older.

This simple trick allows you to wonder about your future life and care about your future self. Visualize yourself several decades from now, think about what your life will be like, and remember that will be you.

To decrease uncertainty about the future impact of your actions, try changing the frame.

It's hard to discipline yourself to avoid things that are bad for you like overeating or being sedentary. So instead of playing defense, turn your daily habits into an affirmative offensive weapon.

- You're not going to get a flat stomach or run a marathon overnight. But can you walk for 30 minutes a day, and switch from a processed snack to a piece of fruit? Yes, you can.

Don't think of this as using up willpower to keep from doing things that are bad for you. Rather, you are taking small positive steps by doing things you like. (And don't worry if you don't initially like the positive steps. After a couple of weeks, you will like what you do.)

Fostering good habits is easier than avoiding bad ones, even if the actions you take are identical.

In your mind, consider your daily habits your secret weapon to drive long-term outcomes one small step at a time.

Be well.

Chapter Thirty

How to Use Metrics Wisely, Instead of Letting Them Manipulate You

Just because you can measure it doesn't mean it's worth pursuing

E xcept for the Friday I drove myself to the hospital for an emergency appendectomy, I never missed a day of work for 25 years.

And I don't even count that as a missed day because I only left work at lunchtime. It was just my luck my appendix waited until Friday afternoon, and I was back to work on Monday.

I confess, I never met a metric I didn't immediately want to dominate. It took me a long time to realize how much chasing success cost me.

I still use metrics in my life, but I'm much more deliberate about which ones I choose. Here's why.

Metrics are fantastic tools ... to manipulate people

You've probably heard this saying: "If you can't measure it, you can't manage it." Makes perfect sense, if what you want to do is manage people.

I'll propose a variation, which is "If you *can* measure it, people will focus on it." That may not sound profound, so let's add this modifier "... to the exclusion of everything else."

My thesis for you is this: your primary focus in your life and at work should be on *looking behind the metrics* that are presented to you by others.

- Challenge your assumptions about what is meaningful.

- Or, if you prefer, just because you can measure it doesn't mean it's worth pursuing.

What's important at work?

This one's easy, right? You are successful in your career in proportion to how much you grow the following:

- Your salary and benefits

- Your titles and promotions

- The number of people you manage

- The size of your budget or business

Depending on your specialization, you will have additional metrics: number of new clients; growth in sales; the number of patents filed, contracts drafted, or lawsuits won, etc.

The point is not the specific metric so much as its very existence.

For what do all these metrics signal? Very clearly, they shout that your success is a function of how much you contribute to things that cause your company to succeed.

Your company's success is not your success (necessarily)

Was I an idiot for focusing on never missing a day's work? Whom did it benefit for me to haul myself into the office when prudence would dictate resting when I caught the flu?

Even if you are a sole proprietor and thus entitled to the full benefits of your labor, you are a fool to set yourself the goal of chasing the same metrics as everyone else.

Why is that you ask?

Because who said the things your company wants are the same things you want?

- What comes with a promotion? More responsibility and stress.

- What comes with a bigger team? More administration and HR tasks.

- What comes with a bigger budget and business? More work and aggravation.

Perhaps some of you are thinking, "Sure, James, all true. But I notice you didn't say anything about the bigger salary. Tell me now why it isn't wonderful to make more money."

What happens to people who orient their lives around money?

When you orient your life around making money, you will likely find ways to achieve your goals. I've seen many people go down this path, only to live frantic, miserable lives, no matter how much they accumulate.

Except for people clawing themselves out of poverty, for whom extra earnings are not only necessary but welcome, it's a rare person who finds themselves genuinely happier when they pursue more money.

Why seek something if it brings you only responsibility, stress, work, aggravation, and unhappiness? Because everyone else is seeking it? That's no good reason.

The only two questions you should ask yourself

1. What do I really want in life (e.g. happiness, meaning, fulfillment, etc.)?

2. What will help me achieve what I really want?

What your company wants and what your colleagues are doing is utterly irrelevant to giving you insight into what you want.

Your only hope in answering these two questions honestly is to put aside for a time the metrics that everyone else is pursuing.

- You may find that it is time spent with your family that brings you joy.

- Or that a generous devotion to your health and well-being makes you thrive.

- Perhaps it is donating your time and efforts to helping others that drives meaning.

Whatever your levers to happiness, I say be blinkered no longer by the metrics others place in your path.

Choose your own goals and let your own metrics guide you.

Be well.

Chapter Thirty-One

My Utterly Romantic Idea of Work

Understanding the beauty of a job well done ... and well paid for

I 've probably worked more hours than you have. This isn't a boast; it's just a fact.

So, how many hours, James? About 85,000. If you can beat that, we should go for a run— we'd probably get on.

I've worked a lot of hours because I've always appreciated the point in them. Once I've got one task done to my satisfaction, I start planning to get the next one done. It's the way I've always lived — I can't see any other way.

True, I've settled down a bit now. I no longer work 100-hour weeks like I did when I started. I've been tapering for a while, down now to my semi-retired 40-hour week. This is a record, especially considering that I am no longer in a salaried job and most of these hours are unpaid.

You would probably hate me if you were my fellow employee — I make everyone else look like sleepwalking slackers. But I'm a nice guy, deep down. I just see this constant shirking of work as immature wishful thinking. Gliding through life without goals, never building savings because spending in the moment is more attractive.

People have called me a Type A overachiever, but I resent that. How can a person who has set regular goals and pursued them with vigor "over" achieve? Think about it. You either achieve your goals or you fail.

I work hard. And most of the time, at least until recently, I received a great deal of money for it. The paid work I do is done with maximum efficiency, which leaves me with maximum time to do the things I consider important. Like write. Or read books. Or spend time with my wife. Or walk.

You must be wealthy!

On a global level, yes. On a Western level, yes. Actually, on any level you consider it, yes. But that's not important. I know friends who've earned very little. My friend Bill worked in minimum wage jobs only so much as he needed to fund an itinerant lifestyle.

Does Bill consider himself poor?

No. He travels to places others have on their bucket lists and lives a simple, satisfying life. He feels guilty that he has free time to lounge on beaches while others are toiling away in factories in the very countries he's bumming about in.

This works for Bill because he's always been able to find temporary work when he needs it. He's healthy and willing to do anything.

It doesn't make any sense to me. How long is he going to be able to keep this up? But according to him, I'm the wage slave stuck in an office while he relaxes in the sun. A fact he often goads me about. Frequently, he tells me how easy life is for him.

Wow! Let's think about that!

This is a guy who's got no credit cards and no bank accounts. He's got no pension and nothing saved for the future. But when I press him on it, he replies:

"But I wouldn't know what to do differently!"

And that's the point! He's spent a lifetime lounging. He likes an uncomplicated existence, without possessions or responsibilities. That's fine. That's his life. Not mine.

Work is only a chore if you don't like what you're doing and if you're not paid well for your contributions. If you have developed valuable skills that people are willing to pay you handsomely for exercising, your profession is a gift.

But a whole generation is coming up in the West with the idea that work is no more than a burden.

They think that was the point of the *Agrarian, Industrial and Technological Revolutions*. For others to generate wealth to free us! And in doing so, freeing humanity — or at least them — from the drudgery of mindless labor, they can enjoy the limited life on Earth they have.

Or did they get that wrong? Is it possible that maybe, someone has to pay for all the elements of society they take for granted?

Sorry. Better get back to work. Someone's got to pay for all this.

Be well.

www.ingramcontent.com/pod-product-compliance
Lightning Source LLC
Chambersburg PA
CBHW060326050426
42449CB00011B/2677